The Wyre Forest Coalfield

The Fowler traction engine Countess, *now restored and residing in East Anglia. This engine was fitted with a winding drum and employed to haul coal and waste at Chorley Woodside drift mine in 1926. The engine was secured in place by setting its wheels in concrete. It was owned and operated by the Griffiths family of Bagginswood. It was at this colliery that the manager, Mr Lebeter, was killed in a roof fall in 1924.*

The Wyre Forest Coalfield

David Poyner and Robert Evans

*This book is dedicated to Fred and Mary Evans
and George and Esther Poyner*

TEMPUS

First published 2000

PUBLISHED IN THE UNITED KINGDOM BY:

Tempus Publishing Ltd
The Mill, Brimscombe Port
Stroud, Gloucestershire GL5 2QG

PUBLISHED IN THE UNITED STATES OF AMERICA BY:

Tempus Publishing Inc.
2 Cumberland Street
Charleston, SC 29401
(Tel: 1-888-313-2665)

Tempus books are available in France, Germany and Belgium
from the following addresses:

Tempus Publishing Group	Tempus Publishing Group	Tempus Publishing Group
21 Avenue de la République	Gustav-Adolf-Straße 3	Place de L'Alma 4/5
37300 Joué-lès-Tours	99084 Erfurt	1200 Brussels
FRANCE	GERMANY	BELGIUM

© David Poyner and Robert Evans, 2000

The right of David Poyner and Robert Evans to be identified as the Authors
of this work has been asserted by them in accordance with the
Copyrights, Designs and Patents Act 1988.

All rights reserved. No part of this book may be reprinted or reproduced or utilised in
any form or by any electronic, mechanical or other means, now known or hereafter
invented, including photocopying and recording, or in any information storage or
retrieval system, without the permission in writing from the Publishers.

British Library Cataloguing in Publication Data.
A catalogue record for this book is available from the British Library.

ISBN 0 7524 1762 2

Typesetting and origination by Tempus Publishing.
PRINTED AND BOUND IN GREAT BRITAIN.

Contents

Acknowledgements	6
Glossary	7
INTRODUCTION	9
1 GEOLOGY	13
2 THE HISTORY IN OUTLINE	17
3 THE SULPHUR COAL IN THE NORTH AND EAST OF THE COALFIELD	59
4 CHORLEY AND HARCOURT	71
5 SWEET COAL WORKING IN BILLINGSLEY, KINLET, HIGHLEY AND ALVELEY	77
6 PENSAX, ABBERLEY AND ROCK	111
7 BAYTON AND MAMBLE	125
8 A RETROSPECT	143
Notes	146
Appendix 1 Gazetteer	150
Appendix 2 List of mines	154
Index	

Acknowledgements

It is almost impossible to list all the people who have helped us in our search for information on the Wyre Forest Coalfield. As far as possible we have acknowledged individuals in the reference list and in the captions to individual photographs. We would like to thank them all for their generous help and patience. Any omission is accidental and we can only apologize to the individuals concerned.

In addition to these people we would particularly to like to record the contribution of the late Pat Barry who worked closely with us in the early stages of this project. His enthusiasm and zeal as a collector were invaluable. The late Geoffrey Bramall and Trevor Stonehouse both allowed us free access to their papers and without these our knowledge of many aspects of the coalfield in the twentieth century would be much poorer. Andrew Santer has given us much valuable information about the mining remains in Hunthouse Woods. We should also thank the staff of the several record offices and other archives we have used. Finally, Mike Moore and Adrian Pearce of the Shropshire Caving and Mining Club provided the spur we needed to translate our notes into this book.

A postcard of Highley Colliery from Station Road, c.1903. The building on the right houses the colliery offices; this has now been converted into two flats.

Glossary

Adit A tunnel driven in from the surface horizontally or at an angle, to reach the coal.

Banksman A surface worker responsible for loading and unloading the cage once it has been drawn up the shaft. (Before the middle of the nineteenth century, haulage would have been by baskets or skips rather than cages).

Basalt An igneous ('volcanic') rock. Basalt found its way into the coal measures, especially at Kinlet and Shatterford (the **Shatterford Dyke**), disrupting the workings and burning out the coal.

Brooch The main seam of coal worked in the north of the Wyre Forest Coalfield.

Coal Cutter A machine to cut the coal mechanically.

Bloomery An early furnace for producing iron.

Drift An **adit**.

Deputy An official who worked underground to supervise the colliers.

Downcast The shaft down which air travels on its way to the coalface.

Fault A break in the underground strata, where there has been a vertical movement of the measures. Consequently any workings that were following the coal would suddenly find that the seam had been displaced (**thrown**), either above or below the coalface.

Heading A (usually) short, blind tunnel, driven into the coal.

Footrid An **adit**, usually for draining water from the mine workings.

Holing The act of making a cut in the coal.

Horse-Gin A simple form of winding apparatus, whereby horses are used to turn a drum, raising and lowering men and materials down a shaft. A **gin-pit** is a pit where a gin was used for winding.

Jig A self-acting incline, usually found underground. A loaded truck descending the incline can pull an empty truck up.

Level In the context of a coal mine, usually a horizontal **adit** (although it can apply to any horizontal roadway in a mine).

Longwall The usual method of working in the Wyre Forest Coalfield. The coal was extracted in one operation, leaving the roof to collapse except where it was held up by timbers and packs to keep the roadways open.

Loader A man responsible for loading cut coal, either into tubs or onto a conveyor.

Pikesman A collier who actually cut the coal at the coalface.

Pillar and stall An alternative form of working to the **longwall** method. The coal would be partially extracted, leaving pillars to support the roof while the workings advanced. At a later stage, the pillars

	might then be extracted ('robbed') to recover all the coal when the workings in the virgin coal had reached their greatest extent.
Plateway	An early form of railway, where trucks ran on L-shaped plates instead of rails.
Roadway	The main underground tunnels of a mine, leading from the shaft to the coal face. These normally carried a tramway.
Shaft Pillar	A large pillar of coal left underground to support the shaft.
Stallsman	A senior miner who agreed to extract a patch of coal along the coal face (the **stall**). He was an independent contractor who would then take on **loaders** to help him. Typically two or more men would share a stall, working as **pikesmen**.
Sweet Coal	Sulphur-free coal, from the **Productive Coal Measures**, found in the north of the coalfield.
Sulphur Coal	Coal with an appreciable sulphur content. It is found in the **Upper Coal Measures**, overlying the Productive Coal Measures.
Sump	An extension of the shaft below the coal, to act as a well to collect surplus water. This would then be removed by pumping or **water-winding**.
Tub	The small trucks used underground at a colliery, each holding about 10cwt.
Tramway	In the context of a mine, the light railway system that operated underground and on the surface. In this book, the term includes the early systems that strictly speaking would be **plateways**.
Upcast	The shaft up which air is drawn after passing around the mine.
Under-manager	At large mines, effectively the assistant manager. At small mines he would act as manager.
Water-winding	A method of draining mines, whereby a bucket (**kibble**) is lowered into the sump at the bottom of the shaft, allowed to fill with water and then hauled up the shaft to be emptied.
Winding engine	The engine (steam or electric) used to move the cage(s) up and down the shaft. It was driven by the winding engineman.

INTRODUCTION

The Wyre Forest Coalfield is one of the Britain's lesser-known mining regions. It covers an area of 50 square miles, mainly in Shropshire and Worcestershire. It has usually been overshadowed by its neighbours; the South Staffordshire Coalfield to the east and the Coalbrookdale Coalfield to the north. In some ways even the much smaller Clee Hill Coalfield to the west is better known than the Wyre Forest Coalfield. However, it has a history stretching from medieval times to the 1970s. In terms of large-scale deep-mining it outlasted the industry in South Staffordshire and for much of the twentieth century it was arguably equally as important as the Coalbrookdale field. While many mines were small and apparently primitive, it attracted its share of dynamic entrepreneurs and innovations; from the seventeenth century when it had some of the first wooden railways in the country, to the twentieth century when it hosted pioneering work on the underground conversion of coal into gas.

Throughout its working life the Wyre Forest Coalfield remained rural in character; only one settlement of any size is found on the coalfield itself and that is no more than a large village. The coalfield takes its name from the Wyre Forest, centred in the middle of the coalfield and one of the largest areas of continuous woodland in England. Paradoxically, there is very little workable coal beneath the Forest itself and almost all the mines were found in two distinct basins to the north and south. Here coalmines were found intermingled with the small mixed farms that typified this part of England. There were periods when the area flirted with other industries; for example at the start of the nineteenth century it was possible to find a blast furnace, forges, a tinplate works, a chemical works and numerous brickworks, limeworks and quarries within the coalfield. Yet widespread industrialization never happened, and agriculture remained dominant. This is not to say that mining did not play an important part in shaping the character of the area; many of the scattered cottages and hamlets were put up for miners and mining certainly did make a significant contribution to the local economy. The pattern of settlements, the roads and paths, land use; these were all shaped by mining. However, this

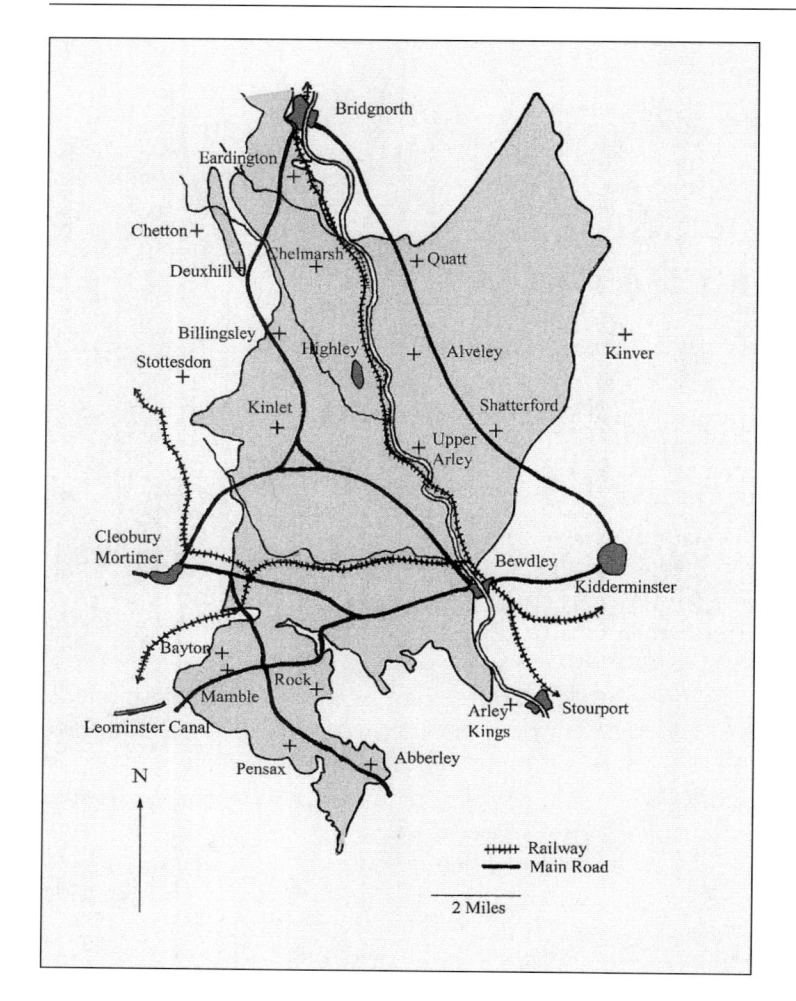

Location of the Wyre Forest Coalfield. This map shows the major settlements within the coalfield, the principal roads and also the Leominster Canal (1791-c.1860) and railway lines (c.1860-1960s).

fashioning of the landscape was subtle and to the casual observer there was little to suggest that the Wyre Forest was a mining district, even when the mines were in operation.

Very little has previously been written about the Wyre Forest Coalfield beyond a few articles and passing references in some books. Written records are scattered and fragmentary. However, with diligent searching it is possible to build up a good picture of the coalfield's history. A fascinating story has emerged; of good and bad times, of technical innovation and incompetence, of visionaries, skilled men, dreamers and fraudsters. All these make up the history of the coalfield and mould the character and geography of this area. After twenty or so years collecting material on the coalfield, we have had to leave much out of this account. Inevitably the illustrations reflect the history of the coalfield in this century and indeed this was when it was at its most productive, but in the text we have also tried to show something of earlier mining. After a brief account of the geology of

Trainee mine surveyor Robert Evans with linesman Pat Ward just up the pit at Alveley in 1953. The trainee surveyor's job was to set out work and measure and record rates of progress of coal faces and tunnels. Surveyors could walk up to ten miles in a day, carrying note books, measuring tapes, tripod and a large brass compass with sights called a Miner's Dial. The surveyors were known to the miners as 'diallers'.

The Bayton Colliery Company's coal lorries at the Gipsy Lane depot in 1926. The company's Model T Ford one-tonners were the first in Worcestershire to be fitted with pneumatic tyres. (G. Bramall).

the area, the overall history of the coalfield is summarized. This includes sections on the technical history of mining, the social history of the mining communities and trade union activity. The rest of the book deals with the individual mines, organized geographically. This is supplemented with a gazetteer of surviving features and a list of most of the known mines. Our main priority has been to document the extent of the industry; much analysis remains to be done.

Our chief hope is that this book will raise awareness and interest in the coalfield. We hope the book may stimulate memories for those who remember the mines at work. We would particularly welcome additional information that they or anybody else can offer (we may be contacted via the publishers). For other readers, there are still many physical remains of the coalfield left to be seen. Without some form of conservation or protection it is doubtful whether they will continue to survive for long. If this book encourages the preservation of some or all of these remains, it will have served its purpose.

David Poyner and Robert Evans
Wyre Forest, July 2000

1

GEOLOGY

The Wyre Forest coalfield straddles the border between Worcestershire and Shropshire, covering an area of some 50 square miles[1]. In a north-south direction it extends from Bridgnorth to the Abberley Hills and in an east-west direction from Cleobury Mortimer almost to Kinver, in Staffordshire. The Worcestershire portion of the coalfield is connected to the Shropshire part by a relatively narrow neck of ground and to the west the Deuxhill Outlier is the largest and most important detached section of the area. For the most part this country is hilly, with deep valleys worn away by numerous brooks and streams in which the coal often outcrops. Until this century there were never any more than villages within the coalfield itself, although the towns of Bridgnorth, Bewdley and Cleobury Mortimer were on its fringes. The River Severn cuts through the eastern portion of the coalfield, but transport away from this remained difficult well into the last century.

The coal measures that make up the Wyre Forest Coalfield are of two distinct types. Over the whole of the southern part of the coalfield, and most of the northern section, the strata at the surface are of Upper Coal Measure age, formally correlated with the Halesowen beds of Staffordshire. Normally, Upper Coal Measures are rarely worked, as the coals they contain are thin and full of sulphur (hence their name of sulphur coals). In the Wyre Forest, this has not been the case, as the seams thicken and improve in quality. In both the north and south basins of the coalfield three important seams are found, but these may not be identical. In the north they are the Brockhall, the Birch Farm seam and the Bank Farm seam. In the south the seams are the Old Hall Bats, the Main Sulphur or Five Foot seam and the Hard coal. It has been suggested that the Old Hall Bats can be equated with the Birch Farm coal and the Main Sulphur with the Bank Farm seam; the Brockhall at the top of the sequence and the Hard Mine at the bottom are postulated to be restricted in their occurrence. Most of these seams have bands of clod interspersed between the coal, and this can sometimes be so thick as to split the coal into two distinct seams; thus in the Bayton area the Main Sulphur exists as the Half-Yard and Three-Quarter coals, which were worked separately. There are also a number of minor seams, too thin to be worked commercially. The issue is further confused by the manner in

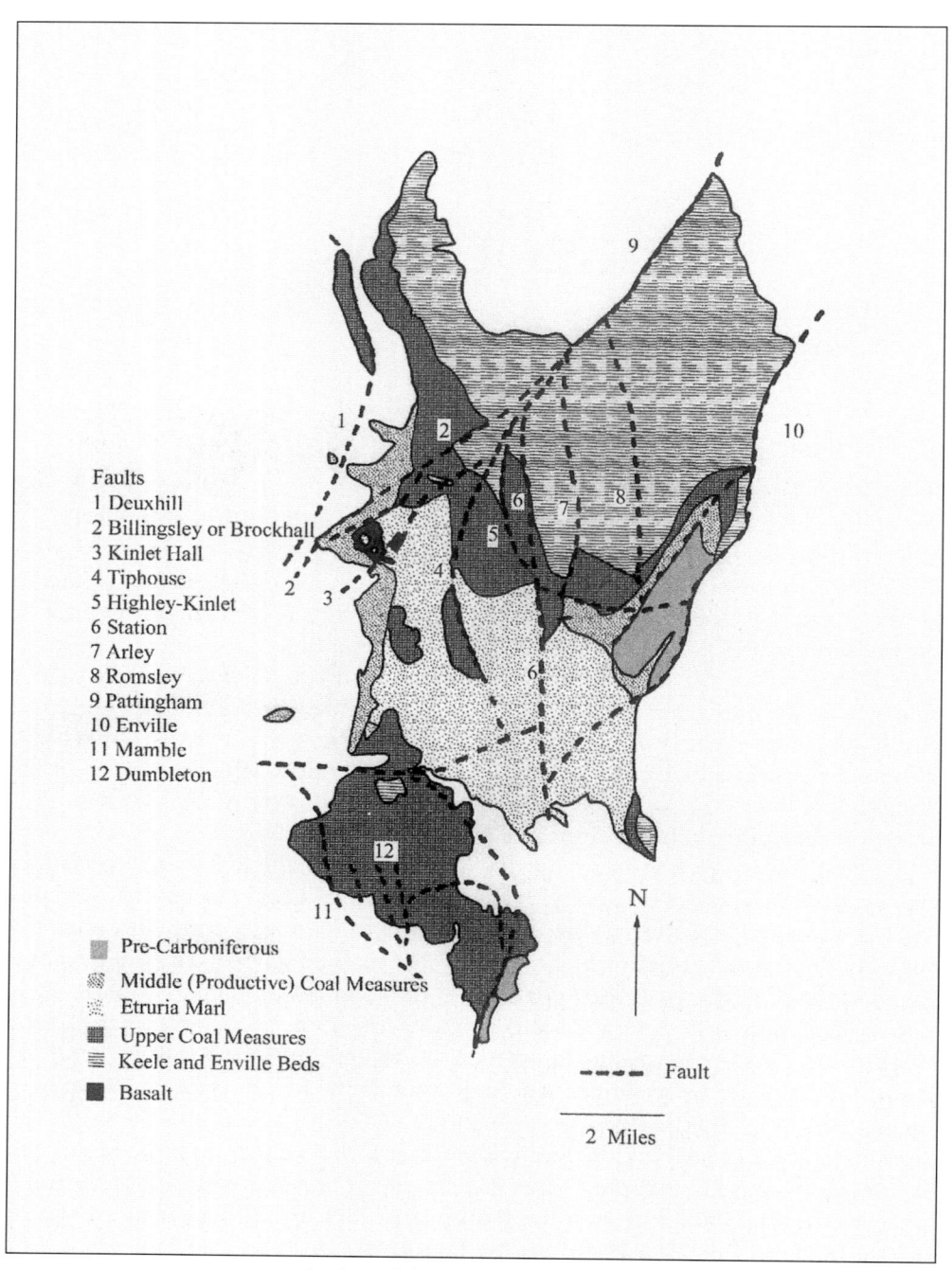

Geology of the Wyre Forest Coalfield.

Seam and strata sections of the Wyre Forest Coalfield.

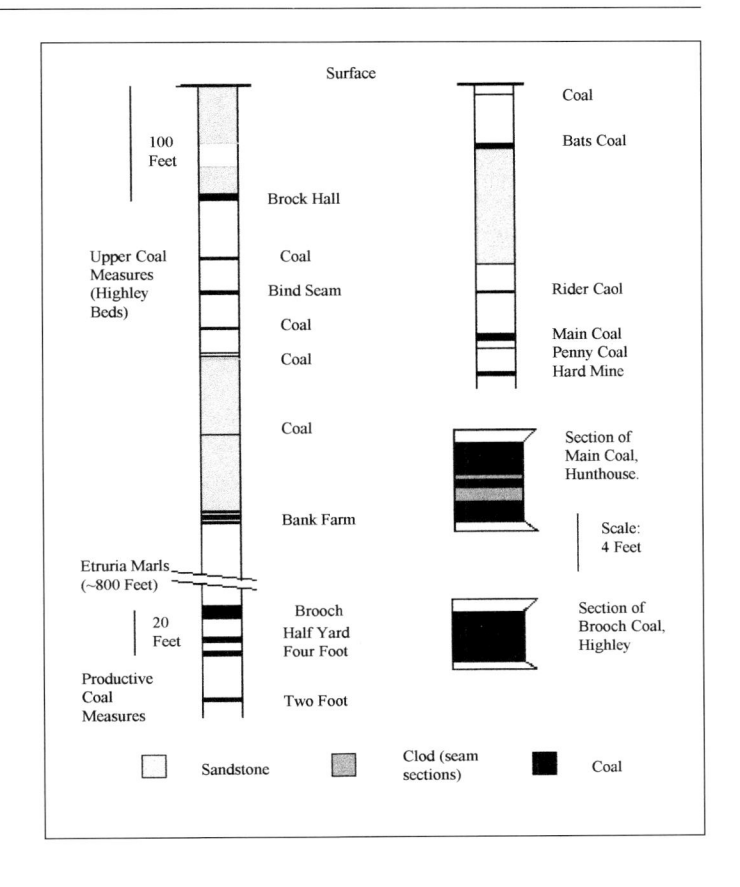

which seams and other strata can rapidly change in thickness and quality over short distances; a fact cursed by both geologists and miners. A number of datum bands exist which have been used in an attempt to make correlations within and outside the coalfield. Chief of these are 'marine bands'; thin layers of limestone rich in the fossil *Spirobis*. More than one of these occurs down the sequence, a fact not appreciated until well into this century, and the cause of much confusion as a consequence. There are also distinctive layers of sandstone (the 'Thick Rock' of the southern basin), mingled marl (the 'Horseflesh' clay) and a band of ironstone associated with the Old Hall Bats.

Of the Upper Coal Measure age seams, the Brockhall was the poorest, not much more than 2ft thick in the north and only rarely mined. The Birch and Bank Farm seams are typically 3ft to 4ft thick, and were more extensively worked. In the south most mining took place in the Main Sulphur, which was up to 6ft thick. The Hard Mine was a particularly tough coal, as its name suggests, and was less extensively worked. The Old Hall Bats has a restricted distribution, but was a commercial proposition in a few places. The Sulphur Coal of the Wyre Forest was sometimes dismissed by outsider observers, especially in the nineteenth century[2]. This was too glib a judgement. Although all the coals had appreciable sulphur content this did not necessarily make them worthless. The sulphur content made the coals unsuitable for iron working, but they could be used for other industrial purposes such as brick making, lime burning and hop drying. The sulphurous nature of the smoke from the coal gave the hops a particularly good flavour and as the coalfield was adjacent to an important hop growing area, this was an important market. The Main Sulphur and Hard Mine also gave acceptable household coals.

The second type of coal measures found in the Wyre Forest are of Productive or Middle Coal Measure age. Middle Coal measures usually contain a number of workable seams of good quality coal (the so-called sweet coals), and this is the case in the Wyre Forest. Four main seams are present; the Brooch or Five Foot, the New Mine or Half-Yard, the Two Foot and the Four Foot. Although these have all been worked, by far the most important is the Brooch. With low sulphur content this was suitable for many industrial purposes, although it was chiefly sold as a household coal. There are also bands of ironstone and fireclay that have been exploited. The Middle Coal measures are only found in the north of the coalfield, and are exposed in an arc stretching from the Dowles Valley to Chorley and Billingsley. Moving further east they are overlain by the barren Etruria Marls and then the Upper Coal Measures.

The geology of the Wyre Forest Coalfield was first investigated at the start of the nineteenth century by William Smith,[3] the 'father' of British geology, and by Sir Roderick Murchison.[4] However, our present understanding owes most to work carried out from 1868 to the start of the First World War by Daniel Jones and Thomas Crossbee Cantrill, with detailed mapping being completed in the inter-war years by R.W. Pocock.[5] In summary, it is likely that the Middle Coal Measures are connected to those of South Staffordshire by an extension projecting eastwards from Alveley. However, as a result of either restricted deposition or subsequent heavy erosion they have a very limited distribution in the Wyre Forest coalfield. In Upper Coal Measure time the Sulphur Coals were widely deposited over the whole of the Wyre Forest Coalfield and extended north to cover the Coalbrookdale Coalfield. These in turn were overlain by the sandstones of the Keele Measures. Subsequent folding and erosion led to the current situation, where the coal measures in the south of the coalfield sit in a shallow basin, with seams outcropping on all sides. In the north, there is a pronounced dip to the east, so that moving in that direction, first the Middle Coal Measures are encountered, overlain in turn by the Upper Coal Measures, and finally the coalfield becomes concealed beneath the Keele beds, later than Coal Measure age.

The coalfield is cut by a number of faults. These predominantly run across a north-east to south-west axis. These have caused much dislocation of the strata, and seriously troubled the mining engineers. Smaller faults are very common, and were a constant source of problems for the miners. In the north of the coalfield there are sheets of basalt, caused by molten lava forcing its way between the strata. These igneous intrusions outcrop at Kinlet and Shatterford, and locally have caused burning and destruction of the coal.

2

THE HISTORY IN OUTLINE

It is not known for certain when coal mining first started in the Wyre Forest. There are no unambiguous references to mining among medieval records; 'coal' at this period could refer both to the mineral and to charcoal. However, coal was certainly being worked by about 1300 in the surrounding coalfields, and it would be perverse to think that the obvious outcrops in the Wyre Forest would have been ignored. At the end of the fourteenth century, the records of Worcester Priory show payment for coal from Abberley, and in Kinlet an area had been known as Le Colliers since the thirteenth century.[1] However, in medieval times wood was preferred as a domestic fuel and industrial uses of coal were few. Accordingly other products of the coalfield may have been more highly prized. In Kinlet, the name Lime Pit Fields is recorded since at least 1565,[2] on an outcrop of *Spirobis* limestone (although whether true underground working took place here is uncertain). Probably the most valuable mineral would have been ironstone. Prior to the advent of blast furnaces in the late sixteenth century, iron was smelted in bloomeries using large hammers to beat the slag out of the ore leaving metallic iron. There is documentary evidence for a bloomery at Neen Savage towards the end of the sixteenth century, possibly in Malpass Wood. By about 1580 this had been replaced by two blast furnaces. These iron-works must have used locally mined iron ore and an extensive complex of ironstone pits survives in Malpass Wood. Between Chorley and Billingsley there are also two bloomery sites with associated ironstone pits and these are probably of medieval date.[3]

While the earliest evidence for mining comes from archaeological records, the first unambiguous documentary references to mining appear in the sixteenth century, and this quickly becomes the main source of evidence. The first such reference is in 1565, when the Corporation of Worcester leased a mine from the Dean and Chapter of Worcester in Pensax to secure a fuel supply to the city to meet a local shortage of wood.[4] In 1594 Thomas Hurd, a local member of the gentry was said to be raising coals at Hollicott, in Chetton, in the north of the coalfield.[5] No doubt Bridgnorth, three miles away, was his main market.

By the early seventeenth century, references to mining in the Wyre Forest Coalfield become more plentiful and it seems likely that outcrop working was taking place over a wide area. Although some of this would be little more than scratching around surface outcrops, there were mines in Chelmarsh, Earnwood and Arley Kings that were of some technical sophistication, probably able to compare with anything in East Shropshire. While it is possible that this increase in recorded mines may be a reflection of better survival of documents, this is unlikely. Deeds throughout the Wyre Forest area rarely mention mineral rights in the sixteenth century, but these are usually explicitly mentioned in seventeenth-century deeds. Landowners were becoming more aware of the value of coal and ironstone beneath their estates. The growth of the coal industry in Tudor and Stuart times is a nationally observed phenomenon and reflects the increasing acceptance of coal as a domestic and industrial fuel.[6]

While there is plentiful evidence for mining in the first part of the seventeenth century, there are far fewer references to mines for the next fifty or so years. Again, this could partly reflect survival of the appropriate sources, but equally other factors could play a part. With the exception of the parishes bordering directly on the River Severn, transport of coal away from the coalfield was very difficult. The coal nearest the surface had a high sulphur content, and the Brock Hall seam in particular is very thin. By contrast the mines in Broseley and Madeley were producing a superior coal adjacent to the Severn. Significantly, during the Civil War, it was these collieries that were the targets of military action to stop coal from reaching Worcester, not those of the Wyre Forest.[7] For an entrepreneur with money to invest, East Shropshire or South Staffordshire would have been a much more enticing proposition than the Wyre Forest. Thus there are grounds for thinking that the expansion of the early seventeenth century did not last, and that the stagnation that was to characterize most of the coalfield for the next 200 or more years began at this time.

In the early eighteenth century mines were certainly at work in Chelmarsh, Kinlet, Pensax, Chorley, Billingsley, Mamble and Abberley. It is entirely likely that a number of unrecorded mines were open elsewhere in the coalfield. However, for the most part these workings would have been on a small scale, and in any single year it is unlikely that the total output for the coalfield would have been more than a few thousand tons; insignificant compared to the neighbouring areas. In Chorley the mineral attracting most attention was iron ore; it was even worthwhile for a time for East Shropshire iron masters to lease reserves here for their furnaces. Generally, however, the iron ore mostly went west to Charlcotte furnace, about five miles away, on the River Rea. From the middle of the eighteenth century coal production probably overtook that of iron as supplies of the latter fell and Charlcotte itself went into decline. However the coal producers faced problems of geology and transport. This can be seen well in the Chorley area, where the sulphur-free coal was a particularly attractive proposition for the miners. Here there were constant problems with faults and water. Even if these failed to deter would-be entrepreneurs, there remained the problem of moving the coal away from the mines to serve a wider area. Morris Thursfield and Lloyd from East Shropshire in the late eighteenth century were said to have found that the local market for coal was no more than a few hundred tons and that the cost of moving the coal outside the immediate area was prohibitive.[8] However geographical isolation was a double-edged sword, as it also made it much more expensive to buy coal in from outside the area. In the north of the coalfield locally produced coal faced competition from river-borne coal from East Shropshire and Staffordshire arriving via the River Severn as well as landsale coal from the Clee Hills: perhaps as a result workings were on a very small scale. In the south of the coalfield it was much harder to import coal from the Severn and there were no competing mines for many miles. This led to a flourishing local industry. However, the level of investment in individual mines was small; the restricted markets did not encourage larger scale mining. Consequently the typical mine would employ only a few men working shallow coal deposits.

Many local miners and landowners were confident that Wyre Forest coal was good enough to supply a wider market if the problems of transport could be solved. The late eighteenth and early nineteenth centuries saw significant attempts at expansion. In the south of the coalfield the Kington and Stourport canal was proposed, running through the heart of the coalfield and opening up large areas of the Welsh borderlands as potential markets.[9] The idea of the canal was first advanced in 1779, but serious efforts to promote it did not begin until 1789 and it obtained its act in 1791. While the promoters envisaged much end-to-end traffic, the collieries close to the canal at Pensax and Mamble were obvious attractions. Sir Walter Blount of Mamble held 1,000 shares in the venture; Thomas Clutton from Pensax took a smaller number. Work started on the central section of the canal, and by 1794 it was open between Southnett wharf (close to Mamble) and Tenbury. The first cargo was coal from Blount's collieries. In some ways, that was the high watermark for the venture, for from then on it was beset by severe constructional problems. There were three major tunnels: Putnal Fields close to Leominster, Southnett just beyond Blount's wharf and Pensax. The first of these was eventually completed, allowing a grand opening to Leominster in 1797; the second collapsed in the middle and the third saw only very limited efforts at construction. The canal was never to be extended beyond the Leominster-Southnett section. However the canal inspired the Pensax Coal & Iron Company to work the mines in Pensax on a much larger scale than ever seen previously (see chapter 6 for details). This venture failed ignominiously, but the canal certainly benefited the Blount family mines at Mamble, allowing them ready access to Leominster and surrounding districts and undercutting the Clee Hill collieries.

In the north of the coalfield the speculation led to more concrete results (see chapter 5). In the early 1790s a group of Newcastle mine owners and businessmen opened a large colliery at Billingsley, connecting it to the Severn by means of a plateway. Within a few years a blast furnace had also been opened. In 1804 the Thompson brothers, ironmasters with interests in the Black Country and South Wales, opened a large mine at Stanley in Highley, on the banks of the Severn. The Billingsley venture was ill-fated, changing hands four times in fifteen years and playing its role in several spectacular bankruptcies (Thomas Telford narrowly escaped ruin as a result of unwise speculation in this venture). Stanley survived for twenty years, most of them apparently profitable. Interestingly, it was Stanley that was working the supposedly inferior sulphur coal, while Billingsley worked sweet coal; good evidence that the sulphur coal in the Wyre Forest was quite capable of holding its own in a wider market with suitable marketing. Both Billingsley and Stanley were large and well-equipped mines. Unfortunately, while they were no doubt splendid to behold, their legacy to the Wyre Forest Coalfield left something to be desired. Nothing on their scale was to be attempted in this region for the next half-century, and this inactivity must in part have been due to the memory of their failure. The disdain of the geologists for the Wyre Forest may well have been born at this time.

For the remainder of the first half of the nineteenth century mining reverted to the pattern of the eighteenth century, with numerous small mines particularly concentrated in the south of the coalfield. In some areas virtually every estate of any size had its own mine and it was common for the mines to be associated with a brickyard. There was some increase in technical sophistication; as small steam engines became widely available they were installed at many mines, although hand winding remained until the twentieth century. In the middle of the nineteenth century around 250 men were employed in around twenty mines. Most of these were concentrated in the south of the coalfield, where in some parishes nearly one worker in three would be a collier. Total output would be perhaps 20,000 tons a year.[10]

The second half of the nineteenth century was crucial in the development of the Wyre Forest Coalfield, as it saw the return of large-scale mining. In this period the national coal industry was growing exponentially; both industry and agriculture were largely buoyant and Victorian prosperity reached its height. Particularly with the memories of the ultimate failures at Billingsley, Pensax and Stanley starting to fade, there was every incentive to open up new collieries. An additional feature was the end of the isolation of the coalfield with the coming of railways. The railways were crucial for the immediate future of the coalfield, for by this time the Severn had long ceased to be a reliable means of transport. The first railways were proposed in the area in the mid-1840s. By the early 1860s both the Severn Valley Railway, running through the coalfield between Bridgnorth and Bewdley, and the line from Wooferton (on the Shrewsbury-Hereford main line) to Bewdley were open.

Initially it was the east of the coalfield that was the centre of attention, as speculators sought an underground connection with the nearby South Staffordshire coalfield (see chapter 3). The famous 'Thick Coal' was cut out by a fault less than five miles from the boundary of the Wyre Forest Coalfield and this periodically exerted a powerful attraction on mining entrepreneurs. From the 1830s to probably the 1860s several boreholes were put down at Compton and in the 1850s there was a substantial sinking at Shatterford. This achieved a measure of success and spawned the only known pottery to work in the coalfield; however, it was ruined by a deep and barren shaft sunk in search of the elusive Staffordshire Thick Coal. The Shatterford Colliery was the first large mine in the Wyre Forest Coalfield since the demise of Stanley.

While there was undoubtedly logic in the hunt for deep seams at Arley, it is harder to see a justification for some of the other boreholes and trials that punctuated this phase of the coalfield's history. The barren measures underlying the Wyre Forest itself were peppered with boreholes and at least one of these was sunk in an attempt to get to the Thick Coal. A minute patch of coal measures at Cleobury Mortimer was treated to a trial sinking.[11] Needless to say this activity brought only disappointment. However the renewed interest did extend to intrinsically more promising parts of the coalfield around Billingsley where the sweet coal outcropped (see chapter 5).

The sweet coal was worked on and off throughout the middle of the nineteenth century at Harcourt on a fairly small scale. The extent to which it extended further east below the sulphur coal was unknown. Most geologists gave little encouragement. Murchisson, the first geologist to describe the strata in any detail in his great work *The Silurian System*, emphasized the lack of any evidence for sweet coal at Highley. He incorrectly considered that the workings at Stanley were cut off by Old Red Sandstone; an important detail as this stratum lies below coal bearing rock in the geological sequence and would have implied that no further coal could exist beneath the Stanley seams. The coalfield was surveyed for the Geological Survey in the 1850s by T.H. Aveline, and Edward Hull in his notes accompanying the survey noted that the nature of the strata in the Highley area was unknown. However, a few years later, in his *Coalfields of Great Britain* Hull, while admitting that the area was unexplored, dismissed the seams as thin and inferior. The trials at Shatterford had the support of at least some local mining engineers, but their failure seemed to seal the fate of the coalfield. In 1869 John Randall, a respected, self-taught geologist from Broseley wrote:

> The long and straggling patches of carboniferous rock, coloured as coal measures on the map stretching from Coalbrookdale to Bewdley where they obtain an imposing breadth are very deceptive in appearance and often raise expectations which only end in disappointments and heavy pecuniary losses. On attaining their greatest breadth at Bewdley they send out an arm in the direction of Stourbridge, as if to claim a relationship with the East Shropshire and South Staffordshire fields; pretensions exposed by sections… of sinkings and borings east of the Severn at Shatterford.
>
> We might multiply instances of attempts to discover workable coals for miles along this worthless tract, by men during the past half century who have sunk fortunes without the least success and who probably received too much encouragement to do so from an unfortunate prognostication indulged in by Warrington Smyth FGS in the memoirs of the Geological Survey.[12]

Ranged against this scepticism from the men of science was the money that would flow to anyone lucky enough to find a substantial area of good quality coal. With profits from coal mines at an all-time high at the close of the 1860s, it was not surprising there were men prepared to speculate. In 1872 a shaft at Billingsley did find a good quality seam of sweet coal. Although a string of companies were formed to exploit this discovery the mine failed to live up to its promise. However, perhaps inspired by the initial success at Billingsley, in 1878 the Highley Mining Company began operations. By now the boom in colliery profits of the early 1870s was well over but the Highley Mining Company found that the sweet coal extended under Highley, several miles from its outcrop in the west. They were able to produce large amounts of good quality household coal and send it away by rail. They flourished and by 1892 were able to start on a

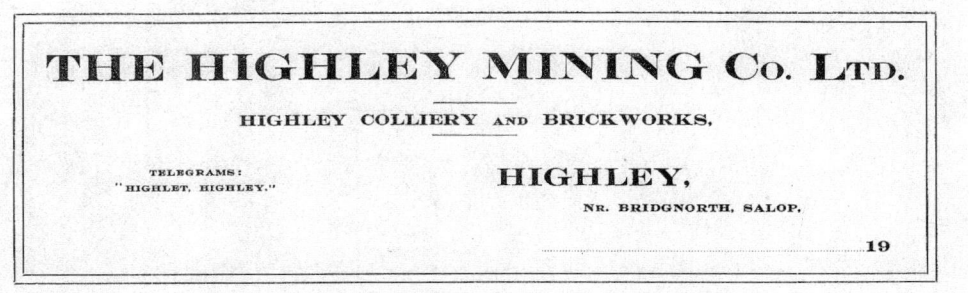

Letter heading, Highley Mining Company, 1920.

Highley Colliery, 1928. The building with the white roof is the new lamproom. The colliery was declared a safety lamp mine in 1927 after a small explosion of firedamp. Candles and open flame lamps were replaced by electric hand lamps and flame safety lamps.

Kinlet Colliery in May 1916. This bucolic scene was photographed by Trevor Stonehouse on a beautiful spring morning. In contrast to this tranquillity, within a few weeks the British Sector of the Western Front was to be engulfed in the Battle of the Somme, where four Highley men were killed. All the surveyors joined the Territorials, expecting to be called up. In the event their services at the colliery were considered to be more important and they were spared the Trenches. (T.H. Stonehouse).

second mine at Kinlet. By 1900 the Highley Mining Company dominated the Wyre Forest Coalfield, producing several times as much coal as every other mine in the coalfield put together. Their demonstration of an extensive area of workable sweet coal beneath the sulphur coal opened the way for large-scale, modern mining. They were to obtain a stranglehold on the north of the coalfield. Although they were briefly challenged by a revitalized operation at Billingsley just before the First World War, this concern soon fell victim to the difficult geology in that area.

In the south of the coalfield the second half of the nineteenth century apparently saw little net growth of the industry (see chapters 6 and 7). In the Pensax and Abberley areas the plethora of small mines that had characterized operations in the preceding centuries all but vanished. The coal around the outcrops had been exhausted and the deeper sinkings needed in the centre of the field would have required more capital than landowners or the small, local coal masters were prepared to invest. Only on the Abberley Estate was there a major new sinking, at Hollins, and this required a partnership between landowner and coal master. By 1900 it stood alone as the only significant mine in this area. In Mamble mining continued to be dominated by the Blount family, but this followed the time-honoured tradition of hand-winding from shallow shafts. Although the local coal masters who worked these mines did well for many years, they were clearly an anachronism at the start of the twentieth century. In Rock the industry showed more signs of vigour for a time. The eastern outcrop of the coal was worked from a series of small but apparently well-equipped mines that seemed to flourish particularly in the 1860s. This outcrop dips much more steeply than elsewhere in the coalfield, and so had not attracted much attention from earlier generations. However, as each farm had its own mine, individual collieries inevitably remained small. By the close of the nineteenth century they had worked out the easily accessible coal and were moribund. At the end of this period there were attempts to amalgamate the mineral rights of adjoining estates and form public companies to develop the area. However, with the best coal already cherry-picked by the earlier mines, these efforts were doomed to failure. The example of Highley inspired a fruitless search for seams of sweet coal in the Worcestershire half of the coalfield, perhaps distracting attention from the fact that the existing sulphur seams produced perfectly acceptable household coal. The end result was that by 1900 mining in Rock was also on the verge of extinction.

Bayton remained to carry the industry into the twentieth century. At the end of the nineteenth century the local Shakenhurst Estate turned away from homebred coal masters to outsiders to work their coal. These brought extra capital to develop the mines; the estate covered several hundred acres and so the coal they were after could be worked on a large scale. From 1910 onwards the colliery in Bayton village grew rapidly, employing around 100 men and producing over 20,000 tons of coal a year. It was only a fifth the size of the Highley Colliery, but it was the largest mine to work in the south of the coalfield up to that time. In 1914 this mine was taken over by the Bayton Colliery Company, who dominated the south of the coalfield as much as the Highley Mining Company did the north.

The inter-war period really consists of the histories of the Highley Mining Company and the Bayton Mining Companies. Although they operated against a period of national recession and the start of the decline of British coalmining they both fared well. There was something of a crisis in the early 1920s; the Highley Mining Company closed Billingsley in 1921 and the old Bayton Colliery closed through exhaustion in 1923. However the Highley Mining Company's other pits at Kinlet and Highley remained profitable and the company were soon looking ahead with a programme of modernization. The Bayton Colliery Company obtained the leases to the Mawley Estate of the Blount family in 1921, giving them access to 1,500 acres of land. Much of this was in the centre of the coalfield and had seen little previous mining thanks to the Blount family's previous infatuation with the small-scale local coal operators. A new colliery at Winwrick's Wood proved very successful. By the

The history in outline

Bayton Colliery c.1905. The downcast and coal drawing shaft is on the right. The aerial ropeway was installed in 1912 on land in front of the upcast shaft on the left of the photograph.

Billingsley Colliery c.1916, showing winding house, headgears and chimney stack. In the foreground is the water storage reservoir. The two-storey building on the right is the colliery offices with the manager's and surveyor's offices on the first floor. Five years after this photograph was taken, the old mine at Billingsley was closed.

THE HIGHLEY MINING CO. LTD.
ALVELEY COLLIERY
NR. BRIDGNORTH
SALOP

Record Week's Output
    Week ended October 7th, 1944 - 5547 tons

Record Day's Output
    September 29th, 1944 - - 1068 tons

The Directors gratefully appreciate the efforts of all employees of the Company resulting in the above Record Outputs and thank you personally for the part you have played in these splendid achievements.

At the same time they have pleasure in enclosing a War Savings Certificate which they ask you to accept with the Company's Best Wishes for the future.

Chairman.

Director.

In 1944 the Highley Mining Company celebrated record coal production by issuing war savings certificates to the workforce.

1930s both the main concerns were expanding again; the Bayton Company with four pits, the Highley Mining Company replacing Highley and Kinlet with a state-of-the-art mine at Alveley.

Although the big two dominated the inter-war years they were not the only players. The 1920s saw a rash of small, short-lived mines at Abberley, Arley and Chorley. In the 1930s this pattern continued in the south of the coalfield but in the north more substantial ventures at Chorley and Shatterford had some success. More coal was produced in the 1920s and 1930s and more men employed in the Wyre Forest then at any preceding time.[13]

After the Second World War the Highley Mining Company and, after a fight, the Bayton Colliery Company were both nationalized. The National Coal Board had no time for a relatively small operation such as Bayton, closing it in 1950. However, they continued to invest at Alveley, with the latter reaching a maximum output of 300,000 tons in 1957. The NCB may have been premature in writing off Bayton, for within a short time they were replaced by a private company who ran a successful mine at Hunthouse for twenty years. The end for Alveley came in the 1960s; a period that saw a dramatic run-down of the industry as coal failed to compete with alternative energy sources. Problems

Alveley pit top in the 1960s, taken from in front of the workshops. The colliery was laid out with lawns and flowerbeds and employed two full-time gardeners. These also looked after the manager's garden (Shropshire Star).

with the latest generation of underground machinery saw the mine closed in 1969. Hunthouse closed due to flooding in 1972. Had either mine managed to survive a few years longer they may have benefited from the revival of the industry brought about by the oil crisis in 1974. Equally, they would almost certainly have succumbed to the second great run-down in the industry in the late 1980s.

Working the Coal

For most of the history of the coalfield the ultimate act of getting the coal relied on the strength and skill of the miner; his ability to swing a pick in a four-foot high space with a candle as his only light. Right up to the 1930s at Kinlet, the job of the man at the face was recognizably the same as his medieval counterpart. Indeed, shovelling coal by hand from the face was still going on in parts of Alveley and Hunthouse almost up to closure. Equally, there were many other technical developments in the industry and Alveley also saw the face machinery that was transforming the job of miner from skilled manual labourer to machine operator.[14]

Kinlet Colliery in the 1930s was the last bastion of pure hand working at the face. It was worked on the longwall principal, where all the coal was removed a strip at a time, from a face about 100 yards long, by gangs of men, each working an area called a stall. Typically one or two men would share a stall; these stallsmen were independent contractors paid piece-rate on the amount of coal they produced in a fortnight or a week. Within the stall they worked as pikesmen, physically cutting the coal; they might employ additional men to help with this work. They would undercut the coal, first working on their knees and then on their sides, to a depth of around 4ft 6in over a 6yd length of the stall. The cut would be kept open by sprags. Prior to the nineteenth century their predecessors had then made cuts along the side of the seam up to the roof and prised the coal down with bars. However, the introduction of powder for blasting had made their lives easier. After 'bottom holing' the coal as described, holes would be drilled by hand in the middle of the face and filled with gunpowder. The charges would be fired by a shotfirer, or perhaps a deputy, and any loose lumps would be levered down with bars known as ringers. The coal would then be loaded into tubs by younger miners known as loaders and pushed by hand to where the road was high enough to accommodate pit ponies. Here they would be collected by the ponies, driven by young lads, and taken to the main haulage roads. The tubs would be clipped onto the wire rope that was attached to a haulage engine and then pulled to the pit bottom, to be loaded into cages and so up to the surface. In the meantime the stallsmen and their labourers would timber their stall and make it safe for the next cut of coal.

In the first half of the twentieth century the lot of the man at the face was transformed with the adoption of electricity and compressed air underground.

Gladys Foster, daughter of Bill Foster the colliery engineer, at Billingsley, in 1922. The colliery closed in September 1921 and the pit ponies were brought out, never to return. They were kept in the colliery field for some months before being sold. (Mrs G. Foster)

Mechanized coal-cutting machines were first seen shortly before the First World War at Billingsley and Bayton. By 1940 all coal produced by the Highley Mining Company was cut mechanically. At Bayton, and in some of the smaller mines, coal cutters were less successful, but compressed air picks eased the mechanical labour. Conveyors were first used for transporting coal at Shatterford in the early 1930s, but were adopted throughout the Highley Mining Company's new Alveley Colliery starting in 1938. In the 1950s wooden pit props at Alveley began to be replaced by hydraulic supports, particularly Dowty Props. In the mid-1960s Alveley saw the introduction of fully mechanized mining on some (but not all) of its faces. Shearers sliced the coal off the face straight onto armoured conveyors, eliminating any need for blasting or manual loading. The faces were supported by 'walking' chocks that automatically advanced once the shearer had taken its cut. The conveyors took the coal to a locomotive-worked railway where it would be loaded into mine cars and then taken to the pit bottom and automatically loaded into the cage. Parallel to the changes in mining machinery, there were also other improvements in working conditions. Candles as illumination at the face were

New Mamble Colliery, 1938. Publicity photograph taken for the manufacturers of Atlas pneumatic picks. The occasion was the first use of compressed air clay spades in a British colliery. Walter Drapier operates the tool while Abner Reece looks on.

Luke Broom operating a coal cutter at Alveley in 1964. By this time the roof was supported by hydraulic Dowty props and heavy corrugated steel bars.

A locomotive is manoeuvred underground at Alveley Colliery in 1964. Ahead is the pit bottom, to the right is the main loco road. This tunnel was 3,000 yards long, dead straight and level and was driven to penetrate the coal lying beyond the Romsley Fault.

first replaced by heavy hand-held battery lamps in the 1920s and then cap lamps in the 1940s. The latter were used with safety helmets, which replaced the traditional flat cap as the normal headwear.

It had certainly been harder for earlier generations. Mechanized underground haulage only seems to have arrived in the Wyre Forest with the Highley Mining Company. In many earlier pits the roads were not high enough for ponies and so the coal was trammed by boys; this continued at Mamble into the twentieth century. Indeed, sledges were still used at Buckets Leasow Colliery at the turn of the century rather than tubs on rails. In the early mines winding would be done by hand or horse gin. The old traditions lasted well into this century, as a hand windlass was installed over a shaft that formed part of the Hunthouse Colliery workings in the 1950s, although it was never used. Hand winding was used routinely in the early part of this century in the

Buckets Leasow Colliery, c.1900. Winding was by hand windlass; these were called 'Jack Rolls' and one stands over the pit shaft in the centre of the picture. This is the coal winding shaft, about 50yds deep. In the background is the upcast and water drawing shaft. In the left foreground is a 'dan'; a box on iron-shod runners used for transporting the coal underground. The baskets on the right are 'whiskets' used to measure out the coal for sale.

Kinlet winding engineman Noah Lawton, c.1915. The enginemen carried out a very responsible job and were usually much respected by the management and workforce. (Mrs M. Price).

Mamble area. Steam winding arrived in the early nineteenth century and was common by the middle of the century. Electric winding was first used in the coalfield at Alveley from its sinking in 1935 onwards.

Drainage of coal mines was always a problem. A simple solution was to sink the shaft at the deepest part of the workings so that all water would flow towards it. If it were then deepened to act as a sump, water would collect in this and could periodically be removed by lowering a bucket or tank down the shaft. This operation, known as water winding, was for centuries the main method of dewatering mines. To some extent it was possible to use small hand-worked pumps to lift water from deep-lying areas elsewhere in the mine to the sump. Another simple method was to drive a drainage level to take the water out to the surface. This was occasionally used, but generally the workings in the Wyre Forest were too deep for this to be practical. If neither of these methods could be used to control water the only solution was to pump it out of the mine. Pumps were some of the earliest machines used in mines, and in the seventeenth century some kind of 'engine' was in use in mines at Arley Kings to control the water. A waterwheel was in use in Billingsley in the late eighteenth century to drive a pump and a little later work was started on the installation of a hydraulic pumping engine. However, this was never completed (see chapters 3 and 5). Steam power was used for pumping long before it was applied to winding, but steam-powered pumps were comparatively rare in the Wyre Forest Coalfield; at the start of the nineteenth century they were used at Billingsley and Stanley and probably also at the 'Engine Pit' in Pensax. The most modern collieries of the twentieth century had powerful electric pumps fitted in their shafts to take the water from the sump to the surface.

Poor ventilation was another of the miner's traditional enemies. The Wyre Forest seams were not particularly prone to releasing gas, although there were a number of small explosions of firedamp and lack of oxygen was always a potential threat. Early mines would have relied on natural ventilation of one form or another to ensure good air was present throughout the workings. In favourable conditions this could be very efficient and was used well into the twentieth century at the mines of the Bayton Colliery Company. A fire bucket was a simple way of inducing a current of air and at Highley a ventilation furnace was present. A fire lit in this would warm the body of air in the shaft causing it to rise, thereby creating a flow. In the 1890s at Billingsley a steam jet in the upcast shaft was used to drive the air.[15] However, effective ventilation usually required mechanical fans driven at first by steam and then electricity as it became available.

In the early mines there is little evidence for anything beyond the crudest sorting of the coal once it reached the surface. Some sieving probably took place to separate out the slack from the larger coal. The slack could be used for burning of bricks or lime, but in other circumstances it would have been regarded purely as a waste product. Sometimes it was deliberately left

The drift mines in Winwrick's Wood by Dumbleton Brook, 1924. George Hill stands in the steel-arched entrance to the loaded tunnel. In the background are the tub haulage incline to the screens and the haulage road to Gypsy Lane. (G. Bramall).

underground. At the end of the nineteenth century more sophisticated screening methods were developed. The sieving was mechanized and the coal was passed along a moving 'picking' belt, where the very young and the very old of the workforce would removes lumps of dirt by hand. The first coal washer was introduced at Billingsley just before the First World War and the technique was re-introduced at Alveley in the 1950s.

The spoil tips from the mine were usually spread indiscriminately around the workings, although in the 1960s at Alveley more care was taken to prepare the ground by replacing a layer of slippery marl with stone. When mining came to an end the spoil was normally used to backfill the shafts. Most mining leases had clauses demanding that the land be restored for agricultural use on the final cessation of mining. This could be done very successfully; a commentator at the start of the nineteenth century recorded how an area of old workings was now plough land of eight or so years standing. Perhaps more common was to crudely backfill the shafts and use the land for grazing. Little or no restoration was done on marginal land, which was simply turned into coppice. Spoil tips have sometimes been quarried for hardcore or occasionally reworked for coal.

An unusual perspective of the spoil tips at Kinlet in 1936. The wooden tubs loaded about 12 cwt of waste stone from the workings, and were emptied down the slopes of the waste tip. The tip at Kinlet extended over a small stream that had been culverted but further tipping caused the stream to back up and form a deep pool that remains today and is known to locals as 'Kinlet Lagoon'. (H. Walker).

The Miners

The first miners were inevitably outsiders to the area, since there would have been no locals with the necessary skills to work underground. The influx of early seventeenth-century miners can be seen in the parish registers of Arley.[16] For most of his parishioners, the priest recorded the full name; however when the first miner was buried in 1608 he was simply noted as 'a collier who hurt himself in ye pyt'. Four years later the next miner to be buried is described as 'John a stranger'. After ten or so years of mining the priest had apparently learnt the surnames of his collier flock; in 1619 he buried 'Pritchet a collier' and in 1622 baptized Thomas the son of 'Lucas the collier'. Finally in 1623 he managed a full name; 'William Morgan, hurt in Mr Duebus cole pitt… was buried'. It seems clear that the miners were regarded as a race apart and this is confirmed by a complaint from the overseers of Arley in 1624 that the village was being inundated with paupers who were putting up squatters' cottages, attracted by the prospect of work in the mines. This feeling of hostility was probably mutual; just over the parish boundary in 1613 the local agent for the mines complained of thefts of coal by the locals from his pits.[17] Most of the colliers are mentioned just once in the registers, indicating that their individual stays in the village were short. Lucas who baptized his son does mark a departure, for he was the first miner who obviously brought a family with him, but in the next few years several other colliers also baptized their children in the local church. A number baptized several children and some of these may in fact have been local men who spent a part of their working lives down the pits. Francis Oates had six children from 1615 to 1624. He died in 1625, the only time he was noted as being a collier. However, Emma Oates, a widow, remarried in 1632 and she was almost certainly Francis's wife. She must have put down strong local roots to stay in the community long after her husband's death. The picture that emerges is of the gradual acceptance of the miners as part of the normal village community.

The example of Arley in the early seventeenth century can probably serve as a model for any place in the coalfield over the next 200 or more years where there was a sudden influx of miners. For example, in Highley at the start of the nineteenth century it appears that the miners who worked at the Stanley Colliery formed their own community, living close to the pit and not mixing much with the locals. An intriguing fact is that the rate of illegitimate births in the village actually fell when the miners arrived; they clearly kept themselves separate! At this time it seems that most miners and their families lived no more than two or three years in the village before moving on to another district.[18]

In some places the influx of miners was so large that they must have swamped the local population. At the turn of the eighteenth century a mine was opened in Billingsley. The population grew from 129 in 1793 (pre-coal mine) to 320 in 1801 and 428 in 1811. Ten years later, when the mines had closed, the population was

The six Ward brothers all worked at Alveley Colliery in 1947. Here Jim, Tom, Bob, Dan, Jack and Bill walk across the pit yard towards the lamp room.

down to 176. The number of houses grew from twenty-three in 1793, to eighty-two in 1811, back to thirty-four in 1821. At the end of the nineteenth century Highley experienced a similar phenomenon, expanding from 400 to 2,000 people from 1880 to 1920. In these circumstances the local population probably had no choice but to mix with new neighbours. Billingsley also illustrates some of the less desirable aspects of this type of expansion. The death rate doubled, the average age at burial was fifteen and for every three infants baptized, one was buried. It is, however, only fair to point out that life was also unpleasant for normal agricultural labourers. Particularly compared with the conditions that existed in the more heavily industrialized coalfields, conditions for the Wyre Forest collier were not generally as grim as might be at first thought. When Highley underwent its great expansion at the end of the nineteenth century, improvements in public health and administration meant that the village was soon transformed into a vibrant small town with shops, services and facilities which were much superior to any of its neighbours.[19]

Where did the waves of new miners come from and go to? Before the mid-nineteenth century it is difficult to trace movements of miners. However, a study of miners at Billingsley and Highley at the start of the nineteenth century suggests that most men came to the area from the established coalfields of the Clee Hill

Three generations of the Westwood family employed at Alveley Colliery in 1947. Grandfather William, son Tom and grandson Derek at the pit top.

Fred Evans of Highley, interviewed by the Bridgnorth Journal *in 1994. Fred started work at Highley Colliery aged fourteen, and during his forty-seven years in the industry carried out every mining job from pony driver to colliery deputy. He retired when the pit closed in 1969. At the age of ninety-two he is the second oldest miner left in Highley at the time of writing (2000), the oldest being Len Giles, aged ninety-seven. Both men consider themselves lucky to have reached such advanced years, having lost many friends and relatives to the scourge of pneumoconiosis – the deadly lung disease caused by coal dust.*
(Bridgnorth Journal).

and Coalbrookdale, and returned there after a few years. A few can be traced to South Staffordshire, and some seem to have been recruited locally or come from elsewhere in Shropshire from non-mining backgrounds. This mix is broadly similar to that seen in Victorian times when data from the censuses are available.[20] Particularly in the south of the coalfield there was much more continuity of mining. Here generations of miners must have grown up and there was probably very little to distinguish them from their non-mining neighbours. In some cases mining dynasties were founded as son followed father; the Craddocks, the Astons in the south of the coalfield; the Winwoods in the north. Some of these men became charter masters, effectively specialist mining contractors who would work the mines for a landowner who lacked the skills to supervize operations himself. Others worked in the mines for a shorter period, before leaving to join the mass of general labourers. From the period of the 1841 census onwards it is possible to build up a detailed picture of a typical miner; although data is not so clear cut for earlier generations there is no reason to think that they did not also conform to the same pattern. Most miners started work in their teenage years. They got

Presentation of long service certificates at the Miners Welfare Hall, Highley, in 1965. Back row, from left to right: L. Warrington, T. Howells, H. Link, H. Brown, C. Palmer. Middle row: T. Griffiths, S. Hart, B. Jones, J. Knowles, B. Woodhall, F. Palmer, W. Turford. Front row: G. Steed (undermanager), S. Childs (NUM), J. Lalley (NCB), G. Wood (colliery manager), H. Pearce (senior overman). (Berrow's Worcester Journal).

married in their mid-to-late twenties to a woman a little younger than themselves and they would raise a family of four to five children. By their late forties they were generally at the end of their active life as miners. If they were lucky they would be fit enough to find other work which would keep them in a decent style. Particularly in earlier times not everyone did this. Cesar Shaw was born in Arley in the late seventeenth century. He moved to the mines in Pensax in search of work. He died aged twenty-seven in 1721, described in the registers as 'a poor collier'. His fate must have been the fear of many generations of Wyre Forest miners, nearing the end of their times in the pit. Only by the end of the nineteenth century was it common to find older men still at work underground as mechanization took some of the effort out of the job.

The job of the miner was inherently dangerous. Although there are no records of any accident claiming more than two lives, deaths were common enough. Typically in the later nineteenth century an average of one man would be killed every other year and this pattern continued well into the twentieth century.[21] However, this must be set against a background of an expansion in the number of men working down the mines; there is no doubt that the larger mines belonging to the Highley Mining Company or the Bayton Colliery Company were significantly safer than their smaller Victorian predecessors.

For every one man killed down the mine, something like 100 would be injured in accidents. Before the twentieth century it was rare to find any medical practitioner living in one of the mining communities and the most a badly injured man could expect would be a trip to hospital in a pony and trap. However, from the turn of the century there was increasing popularity in First Aid classes, with Mine Rescue Teams being formed at the larger collieries. By the 1950s the Alveley Mine Rescue Team was recognized as one of the best in the West Midlands, frequently winning prizes in competitions. Fortunately it was rarely called out in anger.[22]

The ever-present risk of serious injury fostered self-help. A number of sick-clubs were established, where members paid a small weekly sum to qualify for benefits if they were incapacitated. In the early nineteenth century societies were formed in Chelmarsh and Pensax and by late Victorian times they were common, with men either belonging to small local societies or larger national organizations such as the Oddfellows or the Foresters. To give one example of these societies in action, in 1867 Daniel Newman was killed at Blakemoor Colliery. He was a member of the Briton Pride Lodge of Oddfellows based in Bewdley and his widow was paid £20 death benefit. In the 1880s, the Highley Mining Company insisted that all its employees joined the Highley Colliery Ground Club to provide sickness insurance. In 1888 each man paid 6d per week that gave him a weekly allowance when ill and the cost of a surgeon's visit. Of course there was scope for abuse. A judge who investigated the Pensax Sick Club thought that the main beneficiaries were the stewards.[23] For those who did not belong to such organizations there was only charity; when Benjamin Jones, a sinker, was killed at Gybhouse in 1882, the vicar organized a collection at the inquest that raised £2.

Alveley Colliery first aid team, 1939. The Morris Ambulance was kept at the colliery but fortunately its services were little used. Back row, from left to right: W. Amphlett, M. Spruce, R. Evans, F. Broomfield, Mr Hemsley, B. Crowther, G. Pike, N. Link, H. Gauden, L. Turner; front row: G. Hemsley, Mr Caine, Mr Stonehouse, H. Cooper.

Highley Colliery rescue team in the practice gallery at Birmingham University, 1952. Ben Crowther (awarded the BEM for his services to mine rescue) tests for gas. (R. Howe/Sunday Mercury).

The rescue team accompanied by H.M. Mines' Inspector Carver enter the rescue practice gallery at Birmingham University in 1952. The team are led by Ben Crowther, followed by Roy Sargeant, Rol Howe, George Pike, Ray Evans and Norman Link, The rescue team were kept at constant readiness by regular rescue exercises, lectures and tests. (R. Howe/Birmingham Post)

A group of surface workers, stokers and boiler maintenance men at Highley Colliery in 1931. The only man that can be identified is Ted Powell, second left, standing. Shortly after this photograph was taken the colliery engineer was replaced. One of the first acts of the new engineer was to dismiss all the surface workers aged sixty years and over. Ted Powell and most of the men in the photograph found themselves out of a job. (H. Bache).

With the government taking increasing responsibility for welfare in the twentieth century the need for Friendly Societies dwindled.[24]

Aside from issues of life and death, there were many other aspects to life in a mining community. The Friendly Societies had a purely social role besides their contribution to miners' welfare. Club dinners were eagerly anticipated. The local public houses were of course popular attractions. Some individuals inevitably succumbed to temptation; at the turn of the twentieth century it was rare for a sitting of the Bridgnorth Magistrates to go by without at least one miner appearing for drunkenness. There were certainly some who drank themselves into first the workhouse, then the graveyard but these were probably exceptions. Working Men's Clubs were founded in Highley, Alveley and Chelmarsh at the start of the century and rules against excessive drinking were strictly enforced. There were periodic flourishes by Temperance Movements within the mining districts but most individuals probably steered a successful course between excess and abstinence.[25]

There were other attractions besides the pubs. Organized sport became popular in the late nineteenth century. A cricket club was started in Highley in 1883. This allowed miners, officials and even owners to mix together. A stalwart of the Highley Club was Herbert Stonehouse, the Highley Mining Company secretary.

Jack Poyner with his pint at the Castle Inn, Highley, shortly after his retirement aged seventy-six from Alveley where he was the oldest man employed. Born in 1881 on the Clee Hill, he worked variously as a haulier and farm hand, helping his father and at the Barn Pit on the Hill. In 1915 he started work at Kinlet, cycling in from the Clee Hill each day. He was soon called up for service in the war but resumed at Kinlet Colliery in 1918, moving to live in Highley shortly afterwards. On closure of Kinlet he moved to Highley Colliery and then to Alveley. He worked first as an onsetter before becoming the ostler, in charge of the pit ponies. He also worked part-time on the Hag Farm, Highley. When the last ponies were retired from Alveley he drove a haulage motor. Jack lived to be ninety-two; all his sons followed him down the mine.

Alveley Colliery engineering and electrical staff social evening at the Nautical William, Alveley, in 1964. Although their numbers are inevitably depleted, the electricians still have regular reunions. (H. Turner).

As one of the 'owners' his voice carried considerable weight on the field of play. Many years later his son recalled an exchange on a hot summer afternoon between Herbert and one of the ordinary miners who was a fast bowler

'Sir, I'm sure I could bowl much better if I could only take my damned singlet off'

'What, in front of the ladies? Never, I'm afraid.'

Highley Cricket Club became one of the dominant forces in the local leagues. From the beginning of the twentieth century football also enjoyed great popularity; in the Bayton area 'Colliers United' always provided the opposition with a stern test and Highley Colliers (later Highley Miners Welfare) enjoyed equal if not greater success than the cricket team. The football teams attracted large crowds and several local players turned professional. In the 1950s one of these, Gerry Hitchens, established himself in the England team before moving to Italy. In Highley the Shropshire Miners Welfare Fund (a body set up in 1920 as part of a National Scheme) provided playing fields and a pavilion in 1930.[26]

Particularly in the early part of the century, church and chapel played an important role in many miners' lives. While non-conformist chapels were scattered throughout the coalfield, particularly in Highley, the Church of England was probably the most active denomination. Here a series of energetic ministers championed their faith and ensured that church membership included many miners. Aside from regular Sunday worship, weekday evening classes, outings and other social events provided competition to the more worldly pleasures.

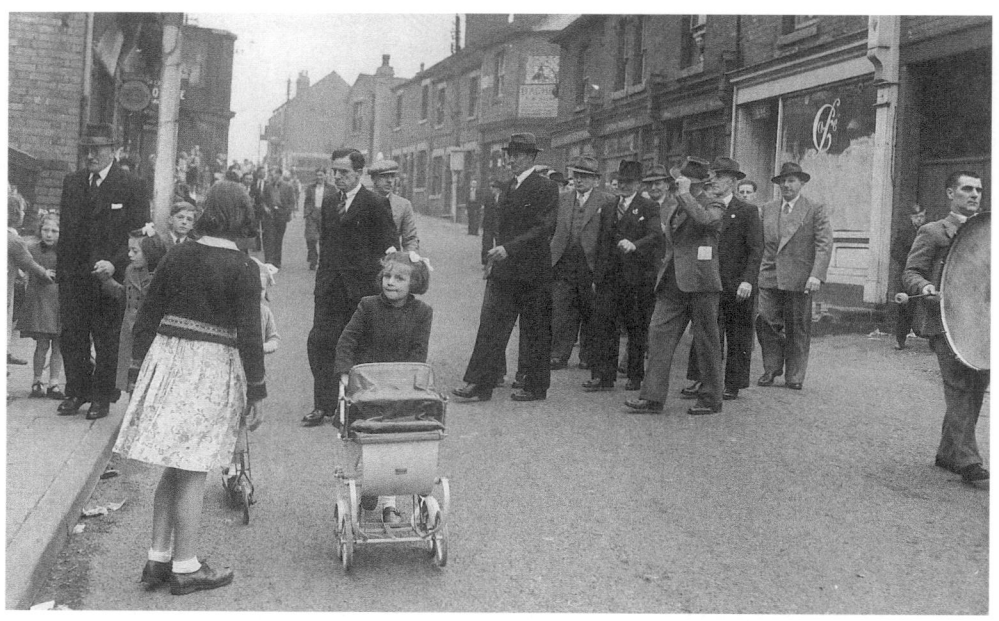

Union officials Sid Childs and George Davies direct operations and Sid Mullard leads the miners as they wheel off to Chapel for a miners service in the 1950s. Len Giles, carrying his drum, follows Highley Brass Band out of the photograph.

Musical evenings and dances were always popular. Both Highley and Alveley had their own bands, and there were a host of other musical groups ranging from hand-bell ringers to ragtime bands. Concerts were put on by the cricket and football clubs, the church and chapels and often ad-hoc committees to raise funds for some cause or other. Dances were popular as a way of meeting members of the opposite sex. Throughout the coalfield village halls were put up to allow events such as these. In Pensax the village hall was largely the creation of Samson Yarnold, the owner of Pensax Colliery. In Highley an entertainment hall was converted to a cinema before the First World War. Thereafter the 'pictures' became a fixture in village life. Some forms of relaxation were simpler. Many miners were keen gardeners and in Highley numerous allotments were available. Home-grown vegetables made a useful contribution to the dinner. Of course, the abundance of rabbits and wild game proved too much of a temptation for a number of individuals. Gambling was another illicit pleasure indulged in by some.[27]

A number of miners put their spare time to more productive uses, having second jobs. Some men had their own smallholdings, often keeping a few cows whose milk could be sold profitably. Others worked as part-time farm labourers. In this rural coalfield many men naturally had the skills needed for agricultural work. Working as pony drivers underground gave many youngsters additional training which they were able to put to good use on coal or other delivery rounds.

Miners and officials on the steps of Highley Methodist Chapel on the occasion of the 1955 Miners' Parade and Service.

Some of the more commercially-minded men or their wives set up small shops in their own homes or in make-shift wooden huts. There were numerous other ways of earning extra money, from acting as a general labourer to sweeping chimneys.[28]

Within any mining community, the miners themselves were always in a minority. Leaving aside the specialist tradesmen, craftsmen and professionals that would be attracted to any sizeable community, there were the wives and children of the miners. It is of course difficult to generalize about the domestic life of a mining family. However, the household chores would almost inevitably fall on the wife. With a typical family of about four children this would probably mean a long, tiring day; washing, cooking, cleaning, shopping. By the start of the twentieth century a woman would probably be expected to work after leaving school; perhaps in service in earlier times, latterly in a shop or a factory in Bridgnorth or Kidderminster. Once married and with children this type of work was almost impossible. However some carried on the struggle, perhaps taking in washing or doing some cleaning. The churches and latterly groups such as the Women's Institute provided some organized social events for the wives. For the children, school gradually became the norm from the middle of the nineteenth century. Prior to this at least some boys must have followed their fathers down the mine at a very early stage, with the

Surface workers on the steps of Kinlet Colliery winding house. Top, from left to right: 'Spider' Matthews (carpenter), Walter Pierce, Noah Lawton (winder); bottom, from left to right: Harold Robinson (smith), William Price, Fred Pepper (banksman). (Mrs M. Price).

Stores compound, Alveley, 1960. Carpenter George Poyner cuts a 12in x 3in baulk with a handsaw. The demise of wooden props made no difference to the work of the pit carpenters, for large quantities of timber were required for general constructional purposes both underground and on the surface. The surface craftsmen were also called to maintain colliery-owned property, such as the manger's house, and could be attached to the 'mobile gang' and sent to help at other NCB establishments. (G.W. Poyner).

daughters set to work on domestic chores. A combination of work and high infant mortality meant that the innocent pleasures of childhood were soon cut short for most infants in mining communities prior to mid-Victorian times.[29]

Industrial relations

There is little evidence to indicate the nature of the relationship between coal owners and miners until the late nineteenth century. Most of the mines were small and worked by contractors employing only a handful of men so that there was probably neither the need nor the scope for formal organization of either employers or employees. Occasionally the mine owners in the south of the coalfield tried to combine to fix a common price for coal. Against this example of co-operation there is also evidence of mine owners trying to 'poach' employees from each other, albeit at a later date. In the early nineteenth century there were large mines at Billingsley and Stanley (Highley) where it might be expected that there would be more tensions between owners and workers. At Stanley the evidence suggests that the employers kept a close watch on their workforce, living close to the mine, owning the local inn and issuing their own money. They probably also controlled the houses where the miners lived and could quickly root out any potential troublemakers. This process seemed to have worked, for the miners at Stanley seem to have remained unmoved while their comrades in East Shropshire rioted in 1821. The isolation of the Wyre Forest Coalfield made it unconducive to militancy.[30]

The thoughts of the early employers about their men are, for the most part, unrecorded. The one exception is Henry Grey MacNab, effectively the managing partner at Billingsley from 1796 to 1802 who was a great writer of pamphlets. MacNab considered miners to be one 'of the most turbulent and ungovernable classes of men in Great Britain'. He complained at the shortage of men, forcing wages up so that the miners could spend a third of their time in 'idleness and dissipation'. This contrasted with the poor lot of the mine owner who 'must … be insulted and seriously alarmed at riots and be frequently tormented by the dissatisfaction and idleness of the very people to whom his adventurous disposition and abilities have afforded employment of the most profitable kind'. Elsewhere MacNab also lamented the 'lottery of mining', how the 'inadvertency of a boy, perhaps not nine years of age who has charge of door connecting with a circulation of air in the mine, may in a moment, blast [the mine owners] hope of wealth forever.'[31]

As will be noted in a later chapter, the hopes of wealth of MacNab's partners were not dashed by the gross irresponsibility of a nine year old boy but by fraud on the part of MacNab. The reputation of miners as a hard drinking and lawless body of men did have an element of truth, at least up to the nineteenth century and some mine owners may have privately agreed with MacNab's sentiments. However it was in neither side's interest to be locked in permanent conflict and examples of industrial unrest are relatively uncommon. Sometimes cases would come to court. In 1878 Edward Evans of Pensax successfully sued his employer, Mr Warren for £1 15s 0d in unpaid wages. In 1859 Edward Blunt, a mine owner at Chetton, obtained judgement against Samuel Matthews, his banksman who had broken his contract by going to work for Edward Crump, a rival owner. Some cases were a little more colourful. Benjamin Trow and Samuel Richards of Baveney Wood were convicted of assaulting Thomas Broom in 1850. Broom had agreed to work for Richards and Trow at their mine but had left after three days. Trow sent Richards to find Broom and together they assaulted him. A case in 1875 shows a rare example of concerted action by miners. It appears that some unscheduled repairs kept eight men in a pit at Pensax an hour longer than normal. They then demanded to be paid a day's wage in compensation. When this was refused they walked out. They were found to have breached their contract by the court. Interestingly one of the men involved was Samson Yarnold, who was to become a mine owner himself in his later years, as well as a councillor and JP.[32]

While there were obviously disputes, it is also possible to find evidence of good working relationships at this period. Edward Ree of Old Hall regularly entertained his men. In an evening in March 1875 they dined on roast beef and plum pudding with ale and cider. There was singing and Reece's health was drunk. Although Edward died shortly afterwards, the next year at about the same time his brother Joseph continued the tradition with a celebration nominally to mark his own birthday. In 1854 Henry Collinson retired as manager of the Arley Colliery Company. The senior workmen organized a dinner for him and presented him with a silver desert basket inscribed 'Presented to Henry Collinson... by a few of the persons under his late management, who regret losing so kind a master'. Events such as these continued until the end of private ownership of the mines. There is no doubt that some owners and managers were held in great respect.[33]

The end of the nineteenth century finally saw the establishment of trade unionism among the miners in the Wyre Forest. It coincided with the reintroduction of large-scale mining, particularly at Highley. It is possible to trace the history of labour relations in some detail from this period onwards. According to one source, the Highley men were incorporated in a union with the Old Hill miners in the Black Country as early as 1883; there were certainly formal links with Old Hill later on. (The leader of the Old Hill miners was Benjamin Winwood who was born in Bayton in 1844, although his family left for South Staffordshire the next year.)[34] As early as 1885 the Highley Mining Company experienced labour problems. Due to a downturn in prices they attempted to reduce wages by 10% at the start of July. At the next directors' meeting at the end of the month it was reported some men were on strike and the manager was authorized to replace them. However, a fortnight later after the intervention of the manager, a deputation of directors met with the men and the wage cut was withdrawn.[35] In September 1887 there was another strike. This was a short but bad tempered affair. It was reported in the local press that the majority of the

Miners' union badges: Old Hill and Highley Miners' Protection Society, c.1910; Miners' Federation Highley, 1931, Salop Miners' Federation, 1919. In the early days the badges were sewn behind the lapels of the men's jackets to avoid recognition of their union membership by the management.

stallsmen went on strike after the company refused to give them an advance. The company prosecuted a number of men for intimidating those still at work. In fact there seems to have been little trouble beyond shouting and throwing of a few stones and five of the nine accused were acquitted. However the following spring the cricket club was reported to be under strength because several of its players had left the village as a result of the strike. It seems probable that the company was victorious in this particular bout.[36] The Miner's Federation of Great Britain (MFGB) was founded at the end of 1889 and in 1893 was involved in a national lockout. The Highley men worked through this, apparently without any trouble. Ironically they themselves went on strike just twelve months later in August 1894.[37] According to the Board of Trade returns, 300 men walked out for a week to retain their old rate of pay. After negotiations with the company they were successful. The report noted that the men were not unionized, explaining why the national strike of the previous year had been ignored. If the Old Hill association had been active in Highley as early as 1883, then its Highley branch had obviously been disbanded within a few years.

A union was certainly in operation at Highley in 1903 and this was ultimately to be affiliated to the Old Hill Association. In July the Highley and Kinlet Miner's Protection Society organized a special day trip to Portsmouth for its members. Over 300 were on this trip, accompanied by '260lb of beef, 155lb of ham, 360lb of bread and 27 casks of ale, mineral water, etc.'; doubtless one of the union's more memorable activities that year.[38] In 1909 politics threatened to rear its head. New legislation restricted the miners' working day to eight hours; although this was something the Miner's Federation had long fought for, there was disquiet in Highley about the new contracts that this would involve. In fact the day after a mass walkout, a meeting voted to accept the new

The Great Strike of 1912. The government were nervous about a million miners on strike and Chief Constables throughout the land were instructed to ensure that events did not get out of hand. At Hollins Colliery Mr Samson Yarnold sits surrounded by a stern group of officers from the Worcestershire Constabulary.

conditions.[39] This was essentially a local dispute; three years later the coalfield was finally caught up in a national strike. The dispute of 1912 was an attempt to gain a national minimum wage and at 2 p.m. on Saturday 1 March the Highley men walked out along with most other miners in the country. Although fifteen special constables were sworn in at Bridgnorth the mood was peaceful; the local paper reported the chief interest was in a pigeon shoot being held the next week. At Bayton, Pensax and Mamble the owners felt it prudent to cease production even though their employees were not unionized and police were deployed outside the pits. The strike had a salutary effect on the Government, who within a month had introduced a Minimum Wage Act through Parliament. In some ways this was the classic compromise that satisfied neither side, for the level of the minimum wage was unspecified and left to District Boards to fix. At Highley strike pay lasted for three weeks before funds were exhausted and by the end of the month soup kitchens had appeared. Work resumed in some fashion at the Worcestershire mines in the middle of March, but at the start of April the Highley men were still out. In fact in a national ballot the membership of the MFGB voted to continue the strike but the union executive, desperate for a way out, managed to call it off. The Highley men returned but then promptly walked out again over what seems to have been a local dispute over conditions of work. Work was not properly restarted until 15 April.[40]

A specially posed photograph taken at Bayton Colliery during the 1912 strike. Jack Blount, with a wheelbarrow of coal, is escorted by a policeman, giving the impression of strike breaking. In fact Mr Blount made his living delivering coal from the colliery with his horse and cart and he supported the miners.

The aftermath of the 1912 strike was to have important consequences. Highley found itself transferred from the West Midlands to the Shropshire District Wages Board for purposes of wage determination. This seemed to work to their benefit; for example loaders at Billingsley got an increase of 1s 9d per day. This did not please their erstwhile colleagues in Old Hill who fared much worse. The Highley, Kinlet and Billingsley miners then severed links with Old Hill to form their own association. The MFGB declined to recognize this and in 1915 Sam Edwards, the Old Hill agent, was asked to contact John Findlay of the new Highley association to organize an amalgamation. Findlay, on behalf of the Highley men, refused to meet with Edwards. In the event the Highley, Kinlet and Billingsley District Protection Society remained independent until the middle of 1918 when the men decided to amalgamate with the Shropshire Miners Association. This was to be an unhappy marriage.[41]

Industrial unrest was largely forgotten during the First World War in the Wyre Forest Coalfield. Eventually the Government effectively took control of the mines and the industry remained under state supervision after the end of the war. During the war the Highley mines remained largely dispute-free and the local union accumulated over £3,000 worth of funds. The end of the war brought the eventual prospect of the coal industry being returned to full private ownership. Unfortunately, at a national level labour relations had not improved during the course of the war and both sides were soon engaged in brinkmanship, even with Government control still in place. The poor outlook may have convinced the Highley men that the safest course was to amalgamate with their colleagues in East Shropshire. The new amalgamated union soon found itself in action. A national strike in 1919 was averted but in 1920 a claim for a 2s per day increase plus assorted bonuses eventually triggered a walkout in October after a series of strike ballots and threats. A local newspaper reported that the initial strike vote in Highley was less than many had expected. This seems to have been wishful thinking as a subsequent vote was seven to one in favour of a strike. After twelve days the miners were given their increase, although even then the vote to return to work at Highley was somewhat grudging (a majority of 135 out of 600). Work also stopped at Bayton, but not apparently Pensax or Mamble, during this dispute.[42]

Although victory was achieved it was short-lived. Nationally coal prices were plummeting and the Government announced that it would be finally relinquishing all control of the mines in March 1921. The owners promptly announced new contracts with reduced rates of pay. Along with almost the rest of the members of the MFGB the Highley men refused the new contracts and were locked out on 1 April. At Pensax, Bayton and Mamble the men remained at work. No strike pay had been paid to the Bayton men in the strike the previous October and they had not renewed their affiliation to the MFGB. At Highley John Findlay claimed the lockout was part of an attack on the whole union movement; an official from the Highley Mining Company retorted that without the new contracts the industry would be unprofitable. Nationally the miners had been promised the support of the railwaymen and the transport workers, the Triple Alliance. Less than a fortnight into the strike the alliance collapsed leaving the miners alone with the coal stockpiled high and the owners and the Government with the upper hand. The Government proposed a £10 million subsidy for the industry, but gave owners the liberty to set the wages they wanted. A vote was eventually taken on this scheme; at a meeting on 19 June, 400 men were urged to carry on the struggle, apparently by the Shropshire executive. Fired on, pickets were dispatched to Billingsley where enthusiasm for the strike was waning to prevent the night shift from going to work. Shortly afterwards some began to question the solidarity of their fellow Shropshire miners. Findlay and Sam Gill, another member of the local executive, set out by pony and trap to Madeley to find out the situation in East Shropshire. Gill's report to the assembled miners on their return was short, depressing and has entered village folklore: 'We know they're at work; we see'd their faces and they were black.'

The Madeley men had apparently accepted the scheme and left the Highley men on their own. At the end of June the MFGB accepted the Government deal and the Highley men returned. It was defeat; the men returned to face pay cuts. Many were left in poverty with all their savings gone. The courts were full of Highley men summonsed for non-payment of rates. Several businesses in the village failed. The final blow came in September when the Billingsley Colliery was closed with the loss of 200 jobs.[43]

There was much bitterness at the actions of the Shropshire Federation. As a consequence Highley disaffiliated from the MFGB and again set up as an independent association. The new union was certainly prepared to show its teeth. In 1923 they took the Highley Mining Company to court over new contracts introduced the previous year at Kinlet and the action met with partial success. Unfortunately, although outside of the MFGB, the union could not escape from national developments. Along with most mine owners in the country the Highley Mining Company tried to introduce new contracts at the start of May 1926, for longer hours with reduced rates of pay. The TUC declared a short-lived national strike to support the miners. This quickly collapsed but the MFGB grimly held out for months in a futile struggle before having to accept the owners' terms. In the Wyre Forest matters were very different. The men at Bayton and Hollins never struck in the first place. At Highley the independent union called a strike and the pits stopped working. After a month the strain was obvious on families that had not properly recovered from the trauma of 1921. In response to an appeal from the Highley Federation the local churches organized collections for the wives and children of the strikers. The Highley Mining Company showed some skill in their handling of the dispute. They themselves donated thirty-five vouchers worth 5s to 10s for the relief funds. At the same time they proposed terms for an extra hour on the day but without any extra pay cut. Although these conditions were rejected by a meeting of the Federation at the end of May, the company opened their pits and within a week 180 men were back at work. By the middle of June the strike was over, with the men working for an hour longer but for the same money as before. It was a defeat but it could have been much worse if the Highley men had still been affiliated to the MFGB. They soldiered on with the strike until November, settling for the extra hour on the day coupled with an average pay cut of 13%.[44]

The biggest casualty of the 1926 strike was the union itself. Its funds had never recovered from the debacle of 1921 when it is said its reserves were used elsewhere in Shropshire. It had been left heavily in debt and was only kept going by a series of loans from local businessmen and sympathizers. Having twice been involved in fruitless strikes its appeal among many of the local miners must have been very limited. It was disbanded and for the next four years there was no union of any kind at Highley. In retrospect it is difficult to avoid the conclusion that its real demise was due to mismanagement of the 1921 strike by Shropshire Federation.

By 1930 most Highley men had decided it was time to make peace with the MFGB. In May of that year it was decided to reform an association and to affiliate to the Midland Miners Federation and hence to the national federation. The Highley and Kinlet Miners Association was soon busy with a variety of work; negotiating with the Highley Mining Company on how to implement national agreements, such as the seven and a half hour day in 1930, or on local matters such as the details of a new contract for cutting coal with machines in 1933. A considerable amount of work was done in the courts, representing injured men seeking compensation. The Highley Mining Company was usually prepared to negotiate with the union although it was noted for driving hard bargains. In spite of the traumas of the 1920s the members of the union were prepared to strike if necessary; a ballot endorsed a call for a national strike in 1935 by 609 votes to twenty-five. In the event Government intervention made the strike unnecessary. However, the union could equally act as force for restraint, preventing sudden walkouts by groups of dissatisfied men. A week's holiday with pay was obtained by the end of the 1930s. The campaign for a closed shop was less successful. On several occasions the union threatened a walkout but always backed down. At times the company appeared sympathetic but on other occasions it took a harder line. A fully unionized work force only came after nationalization.[45]

The Second World War brought some changes to the position of the union. A pit committee was set up as part of a national scheme to help resolve problems. As the war progressed both union and management found themselves increasingly tied together by formal committees as the Government took control of the mines. New technology brought problems; the union asked vainly for coal conveyors to be removed and the old stall system to be restated. There were continuing complaints about non-union labour and there was a threat of a strike ballot over a national wage offer in 1944. This was withdrawn when its legality was questioned. The union had a notable achievement when it secured an extra 2s 8d allowance for Saturday working. However, in 1945 the membership decided to end the union's independent existence when they voted in favour of an amalgamation with the South Staffordshire men. This was in line with the national movement that saw the old Miners' Federation replaced by the National Union of Mineworkers in 1944.[46]

Nationalization brought rather limited changes to the running of the Alveley. The committees and arbitration procedures introduced during the war years remained and grew in significance. There were certainly improvements in some areas and training procedures changed beyond all recognition. However, the National Coal Board was not necessarily any easier to deal with than the Highley Mining Company; one of its first acts was to try and refuse to pay the 2s 8d allowance for Saturday work. In some ways the Highley men enjoyed conditions that were much better than the national average, for example in terms of hours of work and concessionary coal. As demands grew to bring about national agreements the union found itself under pressure for some of these benefits traded away. In the early 1960s it was in open dispute with the Midland Area Council of the NUM over the question of concessionary coal. It was also very aware of the pit closure programme of the 1960s. It was little surprised when in 1967 it began its own unsuccessful fight to save the mine.[47]

In the Worcestershire half of the coalfield the men of the Bayton Colliery Company had rejoined the MFGB by the 1930s, as the Bayton Lodge of the South Staffordshire and East Worcestershire Amalgamated Association of Miners. Membership of the union did nothing to help save Bayton Colliery in 1950 when the NCB closed it down. It must have been particularly galling for the men to read a letter defending the closure decision sent to the local press by J.H. Southall, secretary of the Midland Area of the NUM.[48]

The history in outline

MINERS' SUNDAY AT HIGHLEY

Annual miners parade, Highley 1956. The banner is carried by George Anderson, Ted and Baden Powell and Dan Gauden as they lead the miners to the chapel service. (Bridgnorth Journal).

December 1968. Union lodge secretary George Davies contemplates the announcement of the closure of Alveley by the NCB. (Birmingham Post).

The South Staffs and Shropshire Miners Union banner carried on parades and other formal occasions. The banner is now kept by the Ironbridge Gorge Museum Trust. (Ironbridge Gorge Museum).

From at least the early part of this century some specialized workers belonged to other unions. From the end of the nineteenth century a strict management structure evolved in coal mines. The chain of authority eventually ran from the manager to the undermanager to the overman, finally reaching the deputy or fireman who had certain statutory duties and powers to ensure safe working in an underground district. These management grades had their own associations. Before the First World War the deputies at Highley belonged to the local Fireman's Union and latterly they formed their own lodge in the National Association of Colliery Overmen, Deputies and Shotfirers (NACODS). The surface craftsmen were sometimes also another branch apart. In the 1960s the electricians at Highley became involved in an inter-union dispute when they joined the Power Group outside of the NUM.

3

THE SULPHUR COAL MINES IN THE NORTH AND EAST OF THE COALFIELD

This chapter will review the mines that worked the sulphur coal in the north and east of the coalfield; in an arc from Chelmarsh, Eardington and the Deuxhill Outlier to Arley and Compton in the east and Areley Kings in the south. For the most part these mines were small and relatively short-lived. There were two exceptions to this; the Stanley Colliery on the banks of the River Severn near Highley, and the deep mines at Shatterford.

As noted in the previous chapter, one of the first recorded mines in the coalfield was at Hollicott, near Chetton, in 1594.[1] However, the records of that and neighbouring parishes are virtually silent until the start of the nineteenth century. At this date Thomas Lewis, a local landowner, was working mines in Deuxhill and also Chelmarsh, and there are scattered references to mines in Chetton.[2] Towards the middle of the century a number of collieries became associated with brickworks. At Harpswood, Edward Crump leased a coal and brick works from John Pritchard in the 1850s and 1860s. This had two small steam engines, perhaps one for a winding engine and another for the pug-mill that ground the clay. It is most likely that the clay was dug on the surface at this and similar works, while the coal was mined underground. The slack would go to fire the bricks while the better quality coal could be sold to householders. Crump seems not to have had an easy-going nature: he quarrelled with Edward Reece, the tenant at Harpswood farm, Edward Blunt, a fellow colliery owner for enticing away a banksman for more money, and those of a strict religious persuasion by encouraging his chief brick-maker to work on Sundays (common practice in brick-making). In 1864 when the lease was renewed, a new tenant took over the works; Edward Reece, his old adversary from the farm. There was limited investment in the mine, with an old 4hp steam engine being replaced by an 8hp model, and also the purchase of a Whitchurch Patent Brick and Tile Machine. However, general working practices left something to be desired. In 1868 a miner, Edward Rawlings 'was being hauled up the pit in the usual way when 5 yards from the surface the rope broke and he fell 20 yards to the pit bottom'. Fortunately the water in the sump broke his fall and, when a new rope was found, he was recovered unhurt. Reece

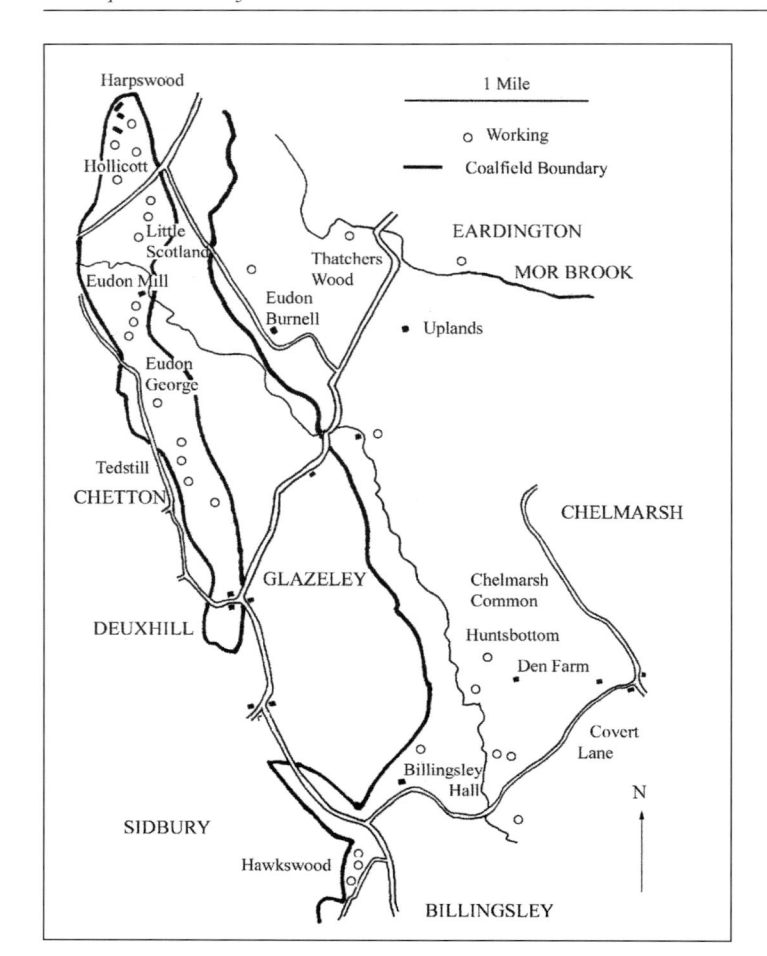

Mines of the Deuxhill Outlier and the north of the Wyre Forest Coalfield, c.1800-1850.

gave up both the farm and colliery in March 1869, and although Pritchard had hopes of finding a new taker, and even brought in Daniel Jones, a professional geologist, to make a report on the mine, nothing further was done.[3] Elsewhere, a similar operation was at work in Tedstill in the 1850s, with a simple colliery working at Eudon George and another at Hollicott. At Tedstill, the works were managed by one James Webster, who left in a great hurry in 1856, leaving the joint owner of the enterprise, Richard Adams, to meet his unpaid bills.[4]

The mines of the Deuxhill Outlier were all in ground that had probably been worked for the preceeding 100 years, but a little to the east at Eardington there was a somewhat more ambitious project. In 1843 Thomas Duppa, the Lord of the Manor, sank an entirely new shaft in the valley of the Mor Brook to a 2ft 3in seam of coal resting on fireclay at a depth of 145 yards. In the course of sinking, limestone and iron ore were both met, raising great expectations. However, neither of these was economic to mine. The mine instead was associated with a brick and tile works and, as at Harpswood, steam power was probably used in both the brickyard and colliery. Eardington was the site of a fatal accident in 1856, which gives an insight into underground conditions. Richard Lyster, a fourteen year old boy, was employed to pull tubs of coal seventy yards from the coalface to the pit bottom. He was assisted by another boy in this task. Working with 2ft 6in headroom, one of the tubs caught the roof and brought it down, crushing Lyster. He died twenty-four hours later of his injuries.[5]

In 1851 a newspaper advertisement proclaimed that the coal and brickworks 'owing to the improved system of management are now in full operation and a large stock of coal [is] always in readiness and on the bank to prevent delay and disappointment to teams coming from a distance. At the brickworks considerable additional machinery and improved kilns have been erected, capable of producing a large supply of bricks, draining tiles etc. of superior quality. A large stock of 2ft and other draining pipes are now on hand. Good stables for the accommodation of teams'

Unfortunately, while Duppa may well have spent lavishly, he apparently got little return on his investments, for his estates at Eardington and elsewhere were mortgaged to the hilt, and after his death he was discovered to be insolvent. Sorting out his affairs proved to be complex, not least because of the illegal activities of one of his executors, Roland Price, a solicitor. Subsequently the mine was sold to Roland Hayward (another solicitor) for £1,000 in 1858, but this sale was contested by Georgina, widow of Thomas, and a battle was fought out in the courts. None of these legal shenanigans could have helped the mine, and it had closed by 1861.[6]

In Chelmarsh, mining was established by the early seventeenth century. At that time the manor was purchased by a dynamic entrepreneur from East Shropshire, John Weld of Willey. In 1631, under the mistaken belief that he was terminally ill, he made a detailed account of all his business interests for the benefit of his son.[7] In Chelmarsh this shows that he had sunk three trial shafts and was certain he was going to find workable coal. He also planned a railway from his works to the river, at a cost of £2,000. As the Brock Hall seam outcrops on the surface at Chelmarsh, he certainly would have discovered coal, although whether he developed his works is not known.

The history of mining in Chelmarsh is then silent until the very end of the seventeenth century. In 1697 Francis Nash, a collier from Broseley, was killed in a pit belonging to 'Mr Nicholas'. It is no longer possible to be certain where this mine was, but it was probably to the west of the parish, close to the outcrop by the Borle Brook. His death did not stop mining, for a 'poor miner' called Charles Shaw is recorded in the Chelmarsh and Billingsley registers until 1701. There are sporadic references to coal miners in Chelmarsh into the nineteenth century, when it was noted, 'there are veins of coal which may be worked without an engine'.[8] Mining of the sulphur coal in Chelmarsh was to continue on a small scale until the middle of the nineteenth century. In around 1880 there was a short-lived revival as a deep sinking was made, but the history of this final venture is intimately tied up with mining in Billingsley and will be considered in a subsequent chapter.

In Highley, mining of the sulphur coal is recorded in the eighteenth century and was generally on a small scale, like the industry in the nearby parishes. However, at the start of the nineteenth century there was a break with tradition with the opening of a much larger mine.[9] This, the Stanley Colliery, appears to have been started in 1804 by John and Benjamin Thompson. A little earlier a large mine had been opened at Billingsley and by this time a blast furnace had been established next to it. The Thompsons were originally from Sheffield but established ironworks in Aberdare, South Wales at the beginning of the nineteenth century. John also developed iron-working interests in Oldswinford and, with other members of his family, helped to establish a forge at Hampton Loade. He would have been well acquainted with the local geography and was probably encouraged by the developments at Billingsley. There is some evidence that the first trial for coal was by an adit, for in December 1804 a man was killed in 'Stanley footrid'. Coal is less than 30 yards from the surface, well within range of a drift. The Thompsons may well have sought either ironstone or coking coal. They found neither, instead getting into the sulphur coal. However, they must have quickly realized that they could find markets for this. The sulphur content of the Main Sulphur seam, which they worked, was not great enough to stop it being used as a household coal and was a positive advantage for hop farmers. The slightly sulphurous smoke it produced was ideal for drying hops. The slack was suitable for burning lime and bricks. By 1807 the Thompsons had their own wharf in Worcester selling 'tops' or best coal at 15s 6d per ton, and 'bottoms' at 14s per ton. This wharf also sold bricks and tiles; the Thompsons were described as brick and tile merchants by 1810. From 1809 another member of the family had opened a lime works in Arley, just downstream from the colliery. John and Benjamin also rented the Heath Farm in Highley, close to their mine. Thus the Thompson family were able to control a series of interlocking businesses from their mine at Stanley.

Benjamin Thompson left the Stanley partnership in 1811 to become managing director of Berwicke Main Colliery in Durham and Fawdon Colliery near Newcastle. He was to have a distinguished career as an engineer and was a pioneer of railways. The next year John sold the mine to William Hughes and Thomas Gritton. John did not have such a distinguished career, eventually going bankrupt in the 1820s, although this was almost certainly nothing to do with Stanley colliery. Of the new partners, Hughes seems to have been the dominant figure. Although from Liverpool, he had formerly been in Worcester where he may have become acquainted with the mine. He and Gritton set about working the business with vigour. They seem to have acquired Birchwood Lime Works in Arley as part of the sale, and in 1813 advertised that this was fully open, with a boatman on duty at Stanley to take the lime to any farm on the river. They also owned Hampstall brickworks below Stourport, probably purchased from the Thompsons. Like the Thompsons, they issued their own currency. In some respects they went beyond the Thompsons' interests. They owned the local public house, two stone quarries in Highley and the large Hextons Quarry in Arley. For transport to their

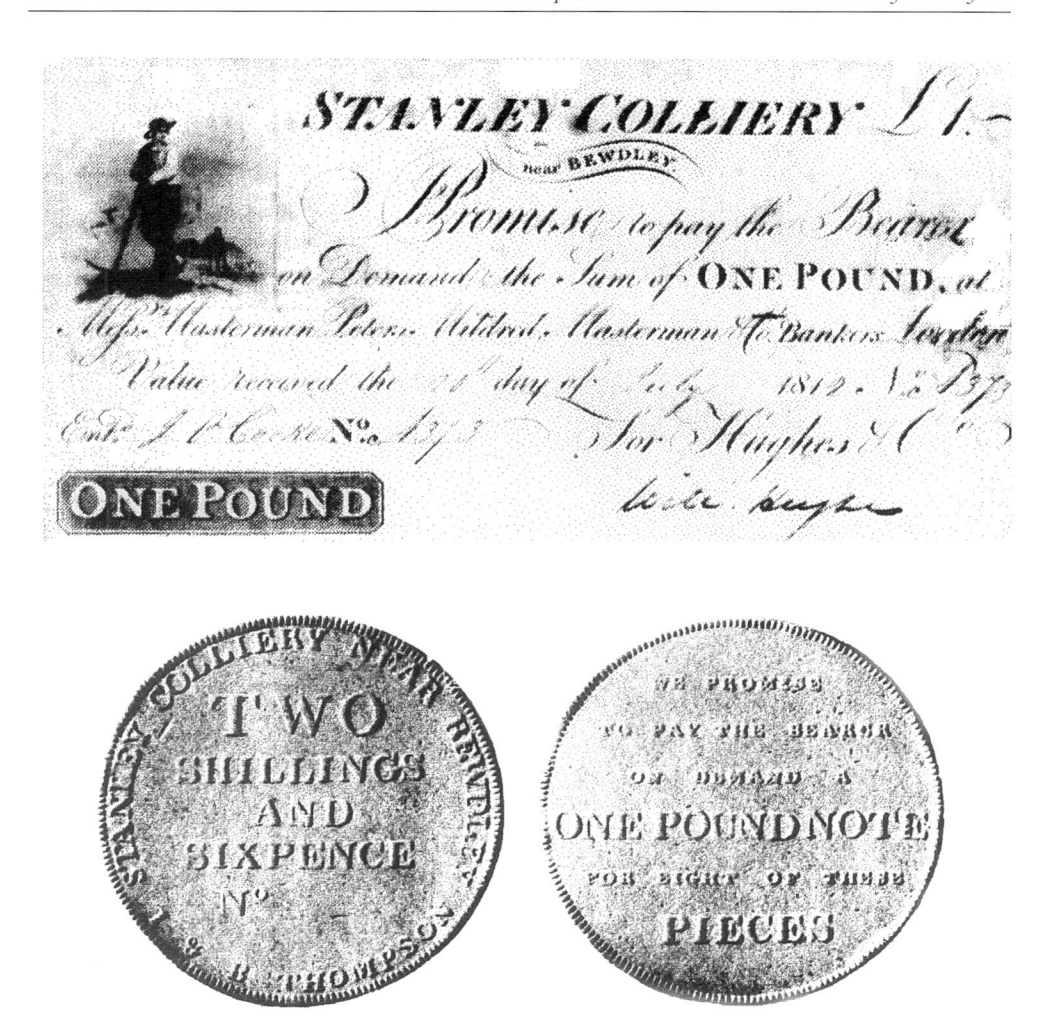

Currency issued by the owners of Stanley Colliery. Top: bank note for £1, issued by William Hughes, 1812;. bottom: 2s 6d token, issued by the Thompson brothers. (W.J. Davies).

Worcester wharf they had two Severn Trows, the *Bridget* and the *Sarah Mytton*, each of 60 tons. Like the Thompsons before them, they leased the Heath Farm, where Hughes lived.

The last mention of Gritton as a partner in the mine is in 1814. In 1816 it was divided into eight shares, two of which probably belonged to William Lewis, owner of the Rhea Farm in Highley, under which the workings must have extended. Although Lewis went bankrupt in 1816, this seems to have had little effect on the colliery, which continued under Hughes's ownership. In 1822 however, the whole of Hughes's empire was offered for sale. It appears that the coal had been lost through faulting. The mine was not an attractive proposition, for it failed to find a buyer and was back up for sale the next year. Still no buyer could be found, so in early 1824 the machinery was sold in lots. Although the mine had been successful for nearly twenty years, nobody thought it worth putting in the extra investment needed to try and find new coal. This was probably influenced by the continued strength of the Black Country industry. In particular, the construction of the Birmingham and Worcester Canal may well have allowed direct competition with Stanley coal at Worcester and the lower Severn. Whatever the reasons for the ultimate failure at Stanley, the sale did Hughes little good, for he was bankrupt by 1826.

Sale notices give some idea of operations at Stanley. There were at least three shafts, one 110 yards deep. Two seams were present, claimed to be 3ft and 5ft thick. The colliery had mineral rights under 180 acres, although faulting probably meant much less than this could actually be mined. Pumping was by a 20hp engine with 120 yards of 8in pumps. There were two 7hp winding engines. Other equipment included 'blowing tackle', winches, 150 pairs of 6ft rails, road and rail wagons. The mine probably employed fifty to a hundred men and boys. For its date, it was well equipped.

Although large-scale mining was to resume in Highley, this was only after a hiatus of fifty years and involved a much deeper sinking to reach the sweet coal.

STANLEY COLLIERY,
On the Banks of the River Severn, between Bewdley and Bridgnorth, six miles from the former, and eight from the latter.
TO BE PEREMPTORILY SOLD BY AUCTION,
BY MR. BENTLEY,
On Monday, Tuesday and Wednesday, the 12th, 13th and 14th days of January, 1824;

ALL the MACHINERY used upon the said COLLIERY, as also the STOCK and UTENSILS of every description;—Consisting of a LIFTING ENGINE, of 20-*Horse Power*, with Boiler, Winch, Blocks, Ropes, and all other necessary Apparatus, with 120 yards of 8-inch Pumps in three Lifts, Working Barrels, &c. &c. complete; also TWO WINDING ENGINES, of 7-*Horse Power* each, with Tackle for the same, and a Flat Rope about 170 yards long, nearly new; a large quantity of Iron Rail-ways, Turnings, Partings, and Sleepers, Coal Waggons, Weighing Machines, Smith's Anvil and Bellows, a great variety of useful Utensils and Timber, suitable for Coal Works, a Thrashing Machine; two well-built SEVERN BARGES, in good repair, one called *The Sarah Mytton*, the other *The Bridget*, each 60 tons burthen, with their Masts, Yards, Sails, Rigging, and requisite Stores, a variety of spare articles suitable for Barges, numerous Tools for the use of the Colliery, Kitchen Range and Grates, a Draught Mare, two Iron Book-cases, Writing Desks, Counting House Fixtures, and innumerable other Effects, which will be fully particularised in Catalogues to be had in due time of Mr. A. Knox, Overseer of the Works; at the George, Bewdley; Talbot, Cleobury Mortimer; Royal Hotel, Bridgnorth; Lion, Kidderminster; Lion, Wolverhampton; and of the Auctioneer, Worcester.

The Sale will commence at Ten o'clock each morning, on account of the great number of lots.

The Engines and Articles used in the Colliery will be sold on Monday and Tuesday; the Barges and Articles connected therewith, Counting House Fixtures, &c. &c. on Wednesday.

Sale notice for Stanley Colliery, 1824

Mining in Earnwood and Arley, 1600–c.1750.

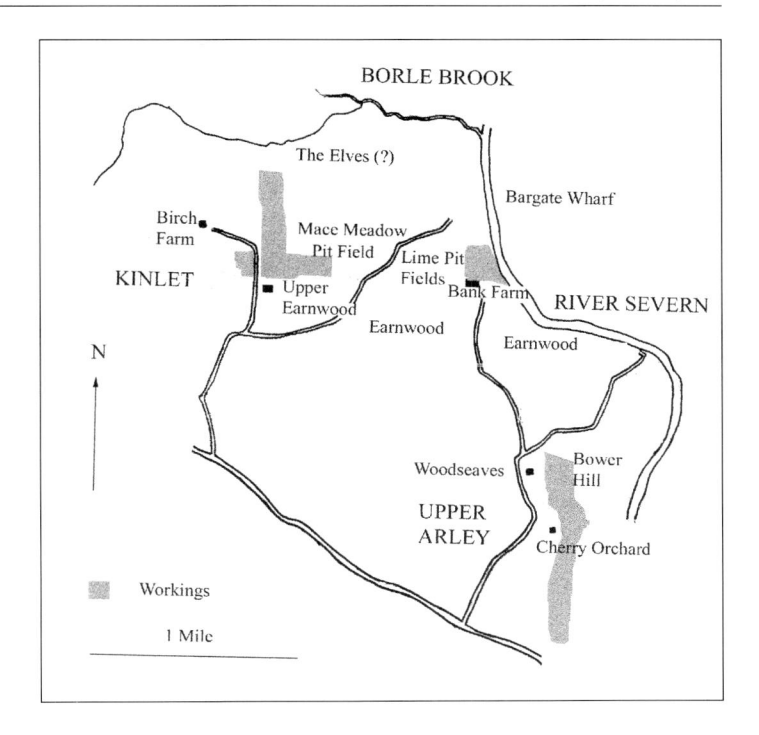

This is dealt with in the next chapter. Small-scale mining of the sulphur coal along its outcrops continued in Highley until the 1850s.

South of Highley lies the district of Earnwood, a tract of land formally within the parish of Kinlet, but which can conveniently be taken to include Arley parish west of the river Severn. Unlike Highley, there is well-documented evidence for intense mining here starting from the early seventeenth century. The Lacon Family had purchased the estate in 1603, and mines of coal were explicitly mentioned in the deeds.[10] Whether they were actually worked at this time is unclear, but certainly by 1608 coal pits were active in Arley, in the area of Woodseaves, where Francis Lacon leased land at Bowers Hill.[11] From this date the Arley parish registers regularly record the presence of miners, either those killed in the mines, or marrying or baptizing children. Lacon had land holdings in the Broseley area where he would have been familiar with mining, and so it would have been natural for him to want to exploit the coal under his land in the Wyre Forest. In June 1613 Lacon leased his mines at Bower Hill and also Lime Pit Fields in Kinlet for nine years to Sir Percival Willoughby of Wollaston, Nottinghamshire and John Slaney, Merchant Taylor of London, and Lord of the Manor of Marsh in Broseley. They also leased a further estate in Arley from a John Brown.[12] Both Slaney and Willoughby were wealthy industrialists. Slaney, in addition to his Broseley interest, was a partner in the Aldenham Blast Furnace near Morville. Willoughby was one of the principal coal owners of Nottinghamshire where his Wollaston Colliery had seen the first documented use of a railway in Britain a few years earlier.[13] Slaney and Willoughby were to pay a royalty of 11d per ton on the coal they raised in the first year, increasing to 12d per ton in subsequent years. Unfortunately problems soon arose. By October 1613 the agent appointed by Willoughby and Slaney, Burton Goodwin, was complaining about Lacon failing to build railways to the mines or erect workmen's' cottages, the poor state of the mines and the propensity of the locals to steal what coal it was possible to obtain. In turn, Lacon petitioned the Lord Chancellor in 1615 claiming that Willoughby and Slaney had in fact raised 2,000 tons of coals without paying royalty, then allowed his mines at Lime Pit Fields to flood, while attempting to obtain the lease of the land at Bowers Hill for themselves. The outcome of this is not known, but it seems obvious that Lacon soon parted ways with his lessees. This is the first recorded dispute over a lease in the Wyre Forest Coalfield, but it was subsequently to be followed by many more. Lawyers were all too frequently the main beneficiaries of mining.

Despite the debacle over Lacon's lease, mining continued to flourish in both Arley and Kinlet. In Arley, other landowners were working mines on their lands and colliers are regularly mentioned in the registers until 1628. It has been noted earlier that particularly those who had to pay for the poor rate in the village did not meet this influx of strangers with universal enthusiasm[14]. In Kinlet, Lacon continued to work coal in Earnwood, in the 1630s and 1640s operating a mine at the Elves with another landowner, Thomas Hammond[15]. This did not generate a mass of legal paperwork and so little is known of it; but it probably produced much more coal than the ill-fated venture with Willoughby and Slaney.

As elsewhere in the coalfield, the later part of the seventeenth century contains few if any references to mining. In Kinlet the next recorded mine is in 1734, when William Childe, the successor to the Lacon Family estates in Kinlet, leased the coal under Mace Meadow and Upper Earnwood to Michael Guest of Bridgnorth for twenty-one years at a royalty of 1s 6d per ton. Childe was to supply Guest with timber for the mine, gin barrels and corves, as well as giving him permission to lay a railway to the river at Bargate. Guest was to supply discounted coal to Childe, not to work more than three pits at once, to restore the land when he had finished mining and not to employ anyone who Childe deemed troublesome. Significantly, in view of the disputes that had plagued the earlier mining ventures at Kinlet and elsewhere, developments in mining law were recognized by the appointment of a banksman to record output, the right of Childe to inspect the works and provision for the appointment of an arbitrator in the event of disputes[16]. The Earnwood mines based around the Birch Farm continued to work until the early nineteenth century. At the start of the nineteenth century they were leased by the proprietors of the Billingsley Colliery and connected to their wharf in Highley by a tramway (see below). This however was a final flourish; the Billingsley venture was soon to end in ignominy and the Birch Mines had probably ceased to work shortly after 1800. Elsewhere in the Kinlet area the Sulphur Coal was

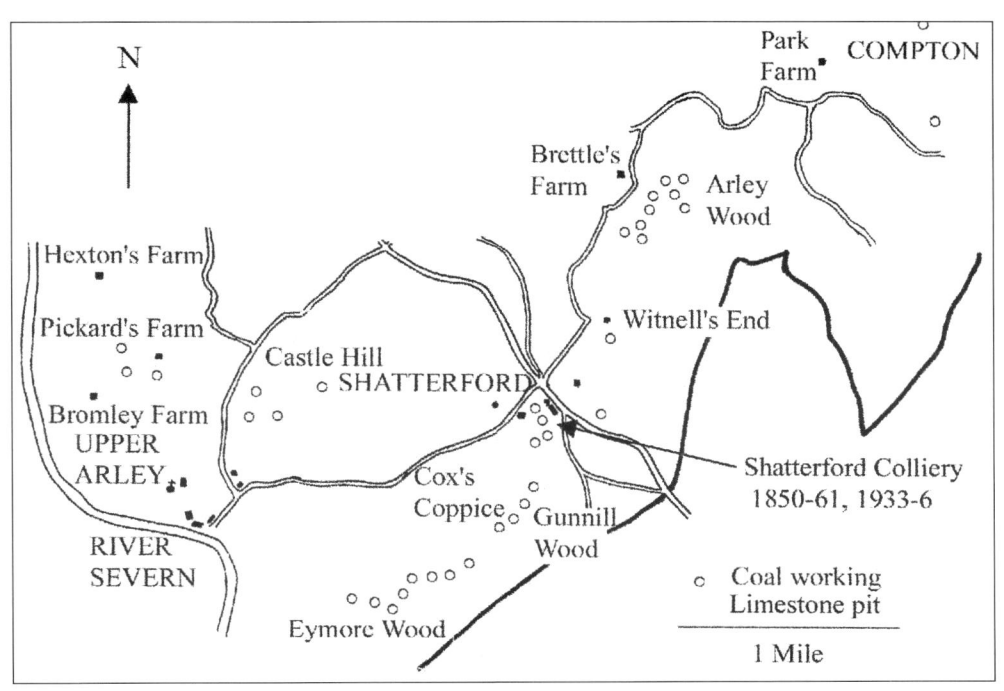

Mines of Arley and Shatterford, c.1850.

worked in the eighteenth century at Little Meaton and Winwoods and Kingswood on the borders of the Wyre Forest. Here too, mining was to continue into the nineteenth century[17]. Winwoods, uniquely for this part of the coalfield, saw an attempt to revive commercial mining of the sulphur coal in the twentieth century. A mine worked fitfully from 1924 to 1927, but it was a very small affair[18].

Details of mining in Arley in the eighteenth century are difficult to recover, but it is likely that there was extensive mining just beyond the coal outcrops. Apparently a deep sinking was attempted during this period but had to be abandoned because of flooding. By the 1830s most activity was focussed east of the river, with the Wagstaff family running a series of pits on the Arley Castle estate of Lord Valencia[19]. These mines were combined with a lime burning business. West of the river there were some sporadic trials for coal, but by now the main industrial enterprise in this locality was a brickworks. In the very far east at this time there were workings in Compton, probably motivated by a desire to locate a connection between the Wyre Forest and South Staffordshire Coalfields. This area had in fact seen largely fruitless trials for coal from 1693. Needless to say, the nineteenth century explorations also came to nothing[20].

By far the most notable venture east of the Severn in the nineteenth century was a coal and clay mine at Shatterford, in Arley. Here the ground is disturbed by an igneous intrusion, the trap dyke, which brings the coal to the surface. However, the coal can be traced further east from where it was worked in shallow pits, and the South Staffordshire field with its famous thick coal was only a few miles away. Although the trial sinking at Compton in the early 1830s had failed to produce workable coal, the rewards of successful speculation in the Shatterford area were likely to be considerable. Accordingly in the late 1840s a series of public companies were proposed to explore the ground here. Initially, none of these took off, until the arrival of one Henry Collinson, a Kidderminster barrister, and Commander Richard Pelley RN of Essex, in around 1850. Collinson purchased an estate centred on Goods Green at Shatterford and began to put down shafts. On the basis of these, he floated the Arley Colliery Company in 1850, with £32,000 capital in £20 shares. This succeeded in raising enough cash to allow the sinking of four shafts (No.2 going down 176 yards to a 2ft 8in seam called the 'flying reed') and the construction of a brick works for red (common) and white (fire) bricks. Three new kilns here cost £156 in 1851. The company also worked a farm on their estate, burnt limestone and ran the Bellman's Cross, an inn[21].

Initially, all went well for the Arley Mining Company. Sales of bricks, coal and lime were buoyant, and timber felled on the estate also made a contribution to profits, which up to 1853 totalled £3,000. The shareholders were rewarded with that rarity in mining investment, a dividend of £1,000. Unfortunately the good times did not last for long. In 1854 income of £379 was set against expenditure of £3,700, and the next year for the first time 'depreciation of plant' caused a paper loss of £11,500. The problems may have been partly geological. The effect of the trap dyke at Shatterford is to throw the coal up at a very steep angle, making it difficult to work. Although Collinson had now retired as manager and apparently cut all links with the venture, Pelley, together with other members of his family, proposed an entirely new company, the Arley Pottery and Firebrick Company, to take over the assets of the old company with £26,000 of new capital. He was thus able to finance the construction of a pottery and terracotta works alongside the brick kilns. This was to be the only example of a large pottery to be based in the Wyre Forest Coalfield; surviving examples of work attributed to it suggest it produced a fair-quality cream-ware. By the end of 1857 the new order was underway. The old Arley Mining Company quietly transferred its property to the new arrival and was then allowed to die without even a proper burial; it was not until 1882 that it was finally struck off the companies register on the grounds that no returns had been received from it for over twenty years[22].

The new money certainly produced activity at Shatterford. The pottery was soon in production and the new colliery manager, John Fellows, carried out reconstruction work to improve working arrangements underground at the mine. However, it was apparent that other developments were in the air. At this time, the prospect of sinking deep enough to find a continuation of the South Staffordshire Thick Coal seized hold of at least some of the shareholders imaginations. The company's capital was doubled, and in 1859 the sinking of a new deep shaft began. It passed beyond the seams already worked, and in 1860, after penetrating 450 yards (the last thirty as a borehole), it was eventually realised that it had all been a disastrously expensive mistake. One reasonable seam of fireclay was found, but no coal worth extracting. The cost of the project must have crippled the associated clay works, for the whole enterprise was demolished and sold for scrap in April 1861. Virtually the last act was the presentation of a silver watch to John Fellows, by his workers, at a special dinner. Contemporary reports concluded with what was so often the epitaph for mining companies: 'the concern finished with the ruin of all involved'[23].

Although Shatterford was the largest of the mid-Victorian mines in this area, mining was also being carried out on neighbouring estates, following the coal outcrop associated with the Shatterford Dyke. Allen Wagstaff, who had formerly worked the coal on the Shatterford estate moved a quarter of a mile due east onto Brettles Farm, where he established a short-lived partnership with the farmer Thomas Wiggan, from 1854. Wiggan sold out to Thomas Woodward of the Arley Castle estate in 1861, who leased the mineral rights under this and adjoining land to Robert Jones, who also owned a colliery at Harcourt (see below). In 1875, Woodward next leased out his estates to Thomas Bertram, a mining engineer previously employed on the Clee Hill. Some time before 1894 a drift mine was opened out in Arley Wood, and in the early part of this century it was claimed that this was operated by a group of workmen who had taken over the mine after the original owner had abandoned it. Whether this was Bertram, who apparently gave up the lease within two years, or a subsequent unrecorded owner is unknown[24].

Mining did not resume in the Arley area until after the First World War. In 1921-1922 the coal in Arley Wood was worked by a shaft and level by a company based in South Staffordshire. At Shatterford there was an abortive attempt to reopen the old Victorian colliery in 1923-1924 by the owner of the estate. Ten years later another attempt at this project did succeed. The Straites Colliery Company cleaned out the old pit bottom, where the timbers were still found to be in good condition. In spite of this, reopening was difficult due partly to the plethora of shafts sunk as part of the old mine. The original workings were found to extend some twenty yards south of the shaft, and initially these were continued. However almost at once the coal began to rise very steeply, and work was soon abandoned. Attention was then turned to the north side of the pit where a level followed a 3ft seam. For a while this went well and a shaker-conveyor was installed underground, the first in the coalfield. The pit was a similar size to Chorley (see next chapter) and, as there, the coal was got with compressed air picks and rotary drills. Although a long-wall face of 30-40 yards was opened up, good conditions did not last. A series of downthrow faults, coupled with a roof made of soft fireclay, spelt the end for the mine. At this point the mine was run by the Kidderminster (Shatterford) Colliery Company, with £15,000 capital and had the presence of Lawrence Holland, President of

Shatterford Colliery 1938. Situated on land at the rear of the Bellman's Cross Inn, the colliery was sunk on the site of an earlier, mid-Victorian mine. The old shafts and pit bottom were uncovered during sinking. The two wooden headgear were served by a steam winder.

the Institute of Mining Engineers on the board. Unfortunately, this was no remedy against unfavourable geology.[25]

To complete the survey of the sulphur coal industry in the north and east of the coalfield it is worth reviewing developments around Bewdley. East of Bewdley a small mine was worked in 1825 by one Samuel Haddock at Lightmarsh. It is perhaps no coincidence that Haddock went bankrupt the next year[26]. Bewdley itself was noted for its brick-making industry in the eighteenth century, and fireclay was worked underground in the vicinity of Dowles[27]. However, the most interesting developments were at Areley Kings, between Bewdley and Stourport. In the early seventeenth century this was owned by the Mucklow family. In around 1620 they agreed to lease the coal under their land to one Thomas Paramore. They agreed to contribute to his costs and indemnify him against loss. Paramore claimed to have installed pumping machinery and to have had forty men at work in his mines, but Simon Mucklow became impatient, stopping the work and dismissing all the men. The ensuing court case reached the Council of the Marches, but unfortunately the outcome is not known. In 1642 a mine was still at work on the Mucklow estates in Areley Wood[28], but it is unlikely to have survived long. In the mid-nineteenth century Christopher Bancks, a Bewdley brass-founder, sank a number of bore holes in this area looking for coal, to no avail, and a small adit was opened up in Areley Kings, probably by the local Zachery family. This may have been intended to supply an adjacent brick yard but could have got very little coal.[29]

4

CHORLEY AND HARCOURT

The coalfield in Chorley through to Neen Savage is one of the few areas where sulphur-free (sweet) coal outcrops at the surface. In early times however, it was the occurrence of ironstone within these seams that was of more interest. Bloomeries at Neen Savage, Harcourt and Chorley tell of probable medieval ironstone mining. Later the ironstone was used in blast furnaces. Ironstone pits at Malpass Wood in Neen Savage could have either served the bloomery, or the two Cleobury blast furnaces of around 1580, located about a mile away. One of the ironmasters associated with these furnaces was John Weston of Neen Savage and in the early 1580s he was also heavily involved in metal mining in Cornwall. It is tempting to think that he might also have worked the Malpass Wood mines. In 1707 the proprietors of Willey Furnace leased all the ironstone in Chorley Coppice from Thomas Crump[1]. Within a few years they had given up their lease after finding an iron supply closer to their furnace, but the Commonheath Coppice mines were then taken over by the Knight family, owners of Charlcotte Furnace, six miles to the north west, near Cleobury North. By the 1730s their area of working had spread to Southall Bank in Billingsley and Scotts Farm in Chorley. The accounts record regular payments to James Cox, who must have been contracted to work the mines. He regularly supplied around 40 tons of ironstone a year to the furnace. The mines were sited along a steeply-sided valley so an adit was constructed for drainage. As the workings progressed, it was easier to sink new shafts at regular intervals than maintain long roads underground. There is ample evidence for this, both on the surface and in the accounts, where money was often spent either on sinking new pits or withdrawing timber from old ones[2].

The mining of ironstone had probably ceased by about 1750, but by then coal mining was assuming more importance. Coal mines in Chorley Coppice are shown on a map of 1754[3] and from that date it is possible to trace the development of mining in some detail (Table 4.1)[4]. Large areas of Chorley, including most of the woodland, were owned by the Crump family and they were the main coal owners. The coal mines were sometimes worked directly by the family in a rather half-hearted fashion. In the 1770s the mines of Thomas Crump in

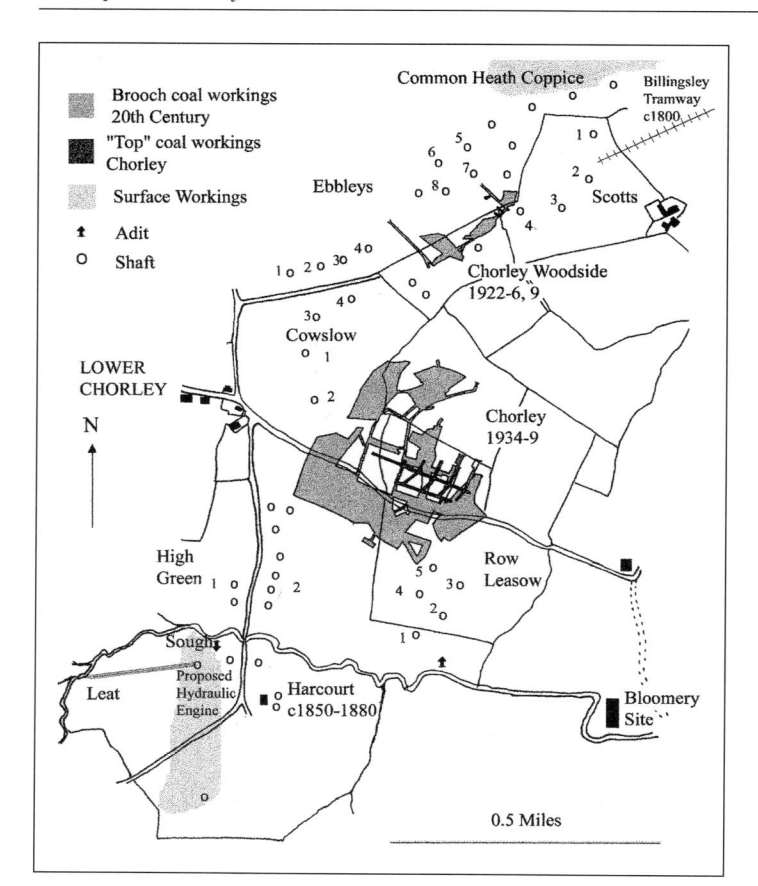

Mining in Chorley. See Table 4.1 for details of the numbered shafts.

Commonheath Coppice were kept drained by the pumping of the collieries on the Billingsley side of Scotts brook. When the leaseholders of these mines gave up them up, they offered the use of the pump (and the waterwheel which drove it) to Crump for a guinea a year. However, he did not consider this to be worthwhile, and as a consequence his own mines were flooded. The mines in the Ebbleys, put down in the 1790s by his son, employed just a single collier underground with a boy on the surface to wind the coal up. They simply supplied coal for the Crump family and the estate. Mines worked on lease were larger affairs. Messrs Morris Thursfield and Lloyd were from Broseley and it is tempting to associate Morris Thursfield with the individual of the same name who developed the Jackfield pottery industry. They found that the local market was only a few hundred tons of coal a year and considered that it was not worth installing the pumps that would be needed to keep their mines dry. Not all of the lessees were from outside of the area; John Malpass was a member of a local family of miners, and Thomas Child of Sidbury was also a timber dealer.

At the end of the eighteenth century the Scotts estate in Chorley was purchased by a consortium of entrepreneurs and colliery owners from the north-east, trading as Messrs Johnson & Co. Their chief interests were on the neighbouring

Table 4.1. Mining in Chorley, 1750-1830

Location	Shaft	Date	Owner	Depth
Common Heath★	1, 2 3	1707 1732-c.1750 c.1740 1775	Willey Furnace Partners Knight family/James Cox Thomas Crump I Thomas Crump II	Ironstone Ironstone 10-12yds
Ebbleys	1 2, 3, 4 5 6 7 8	1778 c.1780 1786-93/4 1786-88/9 1794 1798 c.1820	Morris Thursfield & Lloyd Thomas Crump III	14yds 10-11yds 5yds
Scotts	 1 2 3 4	c.1732 c.1780 1796-8 c.1798 1796-8 c.1797	Knight Family Revd Purcell Johnson & Co.	Ironstone 60yds 36yds 60yds 8-9yd staple shaft
Cowslow	1 & 2 3 & 4	1768-78	John Malpass	36 & 26yds 20yds
High Green Lays	1 2	1766/8 c.1770-80	Thomas Child William Vernon	
Harcourt		1790-3 c.1800-1830	Lady Blount John and Edward Humphries	60yds
Sough Pit		1780-90	Humphries & Fennel	
Nicolls Lane★		1776	Thomas Craddock	
Row Leasow	1 2 & 3 4 & 5	1778	John Malpass	22yds Basset pits
Rays★		1810-15	Mr Gwilt	

★ Shaft not marked on map.

Billingsley estate but they did mine the coal under Scotts, sinking three shafts. Two were relatively shallow but the third was much deeper and used as a sump. To ensure that water drained into this, a staple shaft (i.e. a shaft entirely underground) was sunk to a drainage level that fed the sump. Water was wound up from the deep shaft in buckets powered by a horse gin, the technique of 'water winding'. The Chorley mine was connected to the partners' main enterprise at Billingsley by a plateway that crossed the deep valley of Scotts Brook by means of a wooden viaduct, 60 feet high and 130 yards long[5]. Despite their investment at Chorley, Messrs Johnson & Co. soon went bankrupt, as will be described in the next chapter, and it seems that little mining was subsequently carried out on the Scotts estate. On the neighbouring land of Thomas Crump mining continued until the 1820s but probably stopped sometime after that[6].

Although this western rim of the coalfield was chiefly worked for the sweet coal, there are also outcrops of the sulphur coal in Chorley that attracted the attention of the miners. John Malpass worked an outcrop in Row Leasow by deep shafts and basset pits (the eighteenth century term for a shallow excavation on a mineral outcrop). These were drained by a timber-lined adit. At the start of the nineteenth century the extent of the sulphur coal was investigated by a series of borings extending north and west of these workings, but these do not seem to have lead to any large-scale mining[8].

To the south of Chorley is Harcourt, owned in the eighteenth century by the Blount family from Mamble. As in Chorley, drainage was a major problem. At Lady Blount's mines in Lower Harcourt works were laid out for a 'lever engine'. This was essentially a beam engine placed a short distance underground and worked by hydraulic power. A dam and watercourse were cut to a chamber to house the engine, but the latter was never installed, and the mines were worked fitfully to satisfy local demand. Towards the end of the eighteenth century on the Upper Harcourt estate the coal was worked from the outcrop to underneath the basalt cap of the Knowle Hill in Kinlet by Thomas Craddock, probably a member of the Pensax mining family (see below). However, these workings inevitably had to be abandoned because of flooding. A later partnership of Humphries and Fennell tried to drain the area by means of an adit that emptied into the brook at Harcourt. Unfortunately this proved to be too shallow to dewater any sizeable extent of ground[9].

At the turn of the eighteenth century Harcourt was sold to William Childe of Kinlet; the advertisement details several coal and iron seams, all within 60 yards of the surface. Childe sublet the Harcourt works to John Humphries, who worked them in the first part of the nineteenth century[10]. In 1856 the coal was leased to Robert Jones of Shatterford (see above). Jones appears to have sunk to a depth of 140 yards, perhaps to get below the previous workings In 1876 he renewed his lease, and the provisions of this make clear that the mine was being worked with some care to ensure adequate water and ventilation control. As the eighteenth century miners discovered, water is a serious problem in this part of the coalfield. At Jones's pit it was collected into a sump at the bottom of the shaft;

it is not known how it was removed, but the normal fashion in the coalfield was by water winding. It may be significant that in 1861 a fourteen year old boy was killed at Harcourt by removing the cover of the sump, an essential operation during water winding when a bucket attached to the winding rope would then be lowered into the sump to empty it of water. Harcourt probably employed about twenty men. It closed about 1881, due to problems with water control. Its relative longevity indicates that it was one of the successes of the coalfield. The surface remains suggest that several deep shafts were present[11].

The outcrop of the sweet coal continues south from Harcourt to Bagginswood, where there was mining on the Heath Farm in the eighteenth century, and due south to Baveney Wood[12]. These works continued until the middle of the nineteenth century: at Bagginswood a Mr Robertson, an iron-master of Stourbridge, leased the mines and at Baveney Wood Samuel Richards and Benjamin Trow continued the tradition of the independent collier, getting the good quality Smiths' coal. Midway between the two locations is Brook's Coppice, where coal was worked intermittently in the early nineteenth century, largely for the Kinlet Estate[13].

The twentieth century saw something of a mini-revival of mining in the Chorley/Harcourt area. This was partly a consequence of the closure of the large Billingsley Colliery in 1921 (see next chapter). Some of the officials from this mine became involved in concerns at Harcourt and Chorley. The mine at Harcourt lasted less than a year, but that at Chorley had a longer, if more traumatic existence. Chorley Woodside (to give it its official title) was a drift mine sunk close to the Brooch outcrop in a wood close to High Green. The chief men involved were Arthur Lebeter, formerly manager at Billingsley, backed by David Staley, ex-engineer at Highley Colliery, Fred Pepper, ex-banksman at Kinlet Colliery who had prospered as a result of local property speculation and Charles Home, the landowner. Lebeter acted as the mine manager in day-to-day control of operations. The mine was sunk in the ground that had seen extensive working in the late eighteenth and early nineteenth centuries, so it was always going to experience difficult conditions. Tubs were hauled out of the drift by a traction engine on the surface and air was carried to the face in metal tubes with the help of a fan. The face was very wet and this, together what is said to be the use of poor quality timber props, caused a roof fall in 1924 in which Lebeter was killed. The mine struggled on for a few more years, employing about half a dozen men, until it was finally abandoned in 1928[14].

Chorley soon experienced another mining revival. In 1934 the area attracted the attention of Charles Blewitt and son, brickmakers from Staffordshire. Apparently the Blewitts initially came in search of brick-clay, but it was coal that caught their attention. Notwithstanding the fact that they were in one of the most intensively worked parts of the coalfield, they sank a single small shaft into the brooch seam, with the air brought down in pipes. The coal was sufficiently good for a second larger shaft to be sunk shortly afterwards. Initially the workings followed the coal northwards, up rising ground until old workings were hit. With the new shaft

Chorley Colliery, 1937. The owner Charles Blewitt demonstrates an Atlas pneumatic drill at the coalface for a manufacturer's publicity photograph.

complete, the area to the south was explored. Here the coal was 6ft thick, with a distinct silver sheen, but again plans were thwarted by the presence of old workings, this time flooded. It took a month of pumping to dewater the mine before work started again, this time to the south east. Despite acquiring limited liability status and a nominal capital of £20,000 in 1937, the continued set backs were too much for the mine and it closed in 1939. The final act was to drive a drift to get a shallower seam of coal. At its peak the mine employed about seventy men, with an output of 15,000 tons per annum. On top of the coal was a 6ft thick band of fireclay, which was almost worth mining on its own account. As it was, this was removed by compressed-air picks and the coal then brought down by blasting. The mine was never a serious rival to the Highley Mining Company, but it did provide extra employment for the district and succeeded in recruiting a number of very capable colliers by offering higher wages than the Highley company. A last fling at mining in the neighbourhood of Chorley came with opencast working in 1943-1944, but this was abandoned due to the frequency with which old workings were encountered.[15]

5

SWEET COAL WORKING IN BILLINGSLEY, KINLET, HIGHLEY AND ALVELEY

As noted earlier, the presence of a bloomery on the banks of Southall Bank brook between Chorley and Billingsley points to very early iron ore working in this district. However, documentary evidence for mining does not occur prior to the 1730s, when James Cox was active on Southall Bank, as noted in the previous chapter. Clearly by the late 1770s coal mining was well established in Billingsley with a waterwheel being used to drain the mines (see previous chapter) but unfortunately the owners of this colliery have not been recorded. There then follows a brief unrecorded period until the start of the 1790s, by which time much of Billingsley was owned by Sir William Pulteney, MP for Shrewsbury; a man who owned land over much of the country. Pulteney was an able politician and keen businessman; the patron of Thomas Telford, he would have been well aware of the potential value of the coal beneath his lands. As a national figure, he would have been able to obtain the advice of the best mining engineers in the country and this must have led him to Newcastle to obtain the services of George Johnson. Johnson was one of the premier colliery viewers (i.e. engineers) in the land, with international experience as a consultant. By 1794 Johnson had put together a consortium of Newcastle-based landowners and professionals to lease the coal under Pulteney's land. His backers included William Chapman, a noted engineer; Sir John Gray, an MP and most significantly Henry Gray MacNab, his brother-in-law. Trained at St Andrews University as a physician, by the early 1790s MacNab was established as an influential figure in the north-eastern coal trade, with a number of pamphlets to his name. In June 1794 the draft leases were signed, and soon work began at Billingsley, initially using at least some men brought down especially from the north-east[1].

One of the first problems the partnership had to overcome was the lack of effective transport in the area. Billingsley was on the Bridgnorth-Cleobury Turnpike, but that was not suitable for heavy coal traffic. A way had to be found to move the coal onto the River Severn. The first idea was for a canal, partly along the Borle Brook, possibly with an extension all the way to the lime works at Oreton. It was at this point that a future thorn in the side of the works first

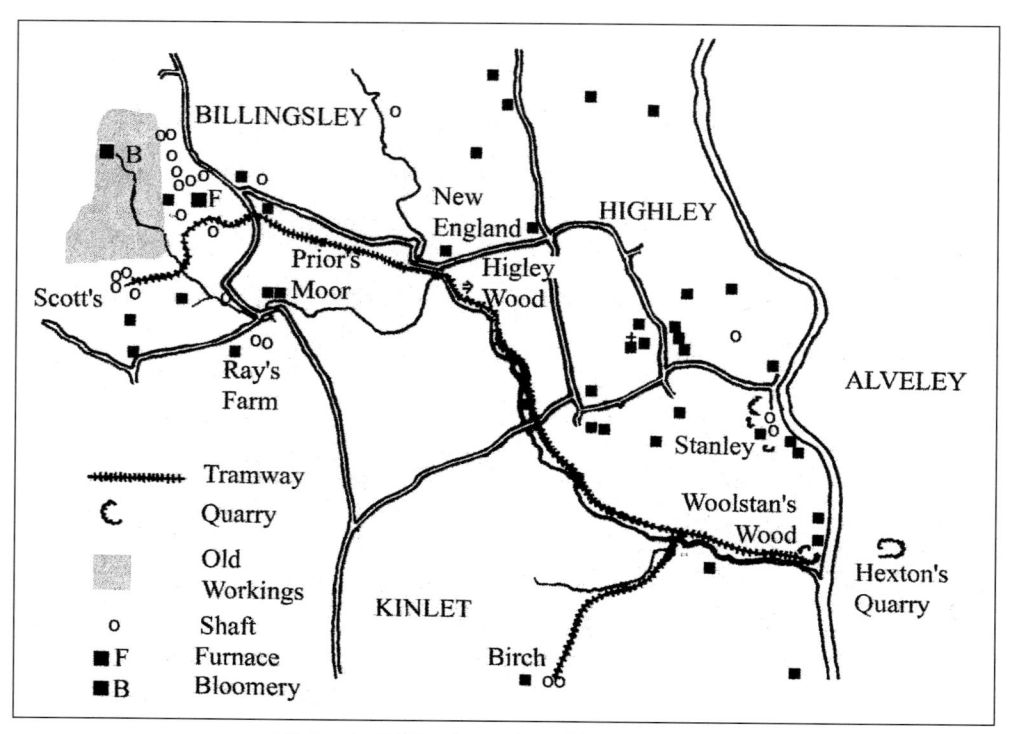

Mining in Billingsley and Highley, 1790-1825.

became apparent, with the implacable opposition of William Lacon Childe to the mine. Childe's property bordered Pulteney's estate on the south; more significantly he controlled the only practical route from Billingsley to the Severn at Highley. The canalization of the Borle needed his wholesale co-operation, and this was not forthcoming. Childe's motives for opposing the mines are not entirely obvious; he was not against collieries *per se*, as he had small working mines on his own estate. He claimed that the large mine at Billingsley could force these to close, ultimately forcing up the price of coal in the district. Childe was also a committed countryman. He was in the forefront of agricultural improvement and was a keen huntsman. He may have feared the impact of large-scale mining on all of this. Whatever his motives, he succeeded in killing off the canal. Instead the partners constructed a horse-operated plateway, following the line of the Borle Brook but as far as possible on the opposite side of the bank from Childe's land. Even this was not entirely possible, for in Highley they did have to cross through a short section of his land. Childe drove a hard bargain, for he made the Partners lease the Birch Colliery and connect it to their plateway by means of a branch. As the Birch was a small mine working the sulphur coal (Chapter 3), it was of no value to Johnson & Co., but they had little choice in the matter[2].

Fortunately other landowners were not as obstructive as Childe, and Johnson & Co. were able to lease or purchase a number of additional estates that they thought

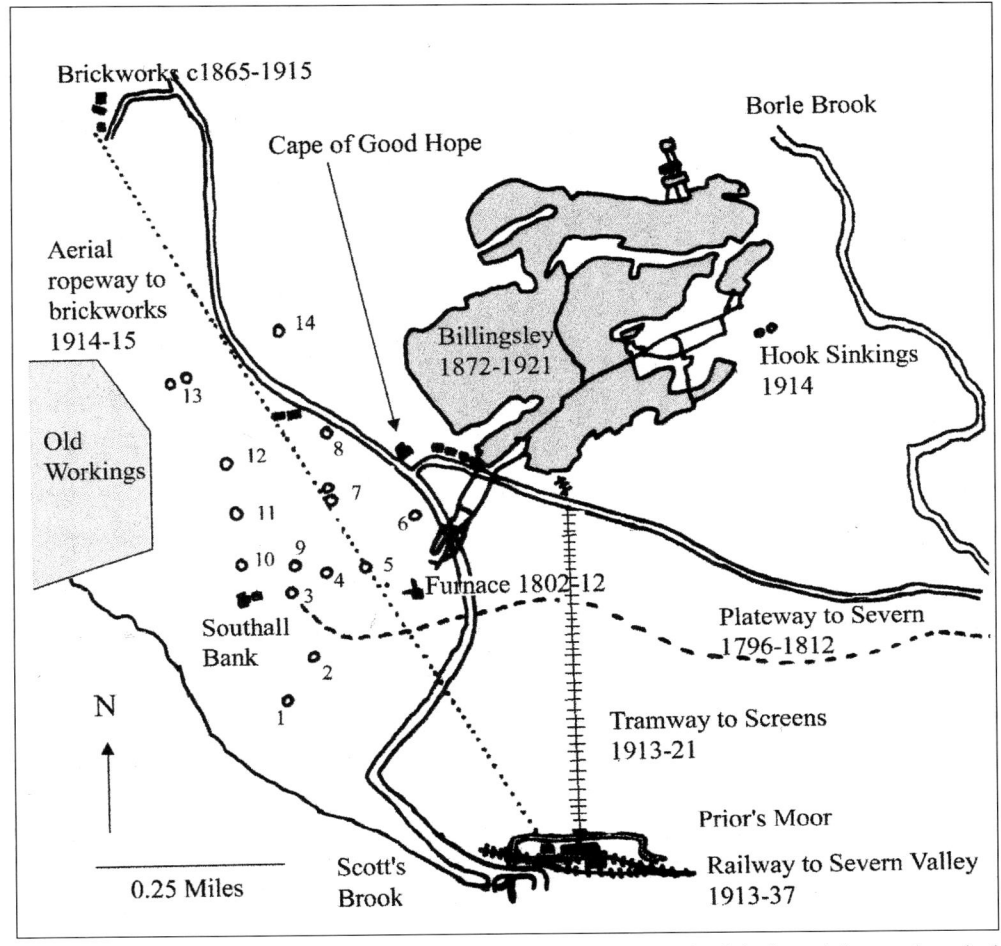

Shafts at Billingsley. Shaded areas are underground workings. Details of shafts: sulphur coal worked at 2, 4, 6, 8, 13; brooch worked at 3-7, 9-13; ironstone worked at 3, 4; no coal worked at 1 (200yds, barren) and 14 (30yds, abandoned after dispute with landlord). Shafts at 7 used for pumping up to a level which then drained to brook. Billingsley No.1 shaft sunk 1872, No.2 shaft sunk 1875 using shallow shaft of 1811.

would strengthen their position. In Chorley they purchased the Scotts estate where they worked the coal. As noted earlier, these mines were connected to the Billingsley works and the tramway to the River Severn by a spectacular wooden bridge[3]. In Highley they purchased the New England estate where their plateway crossed the Borle Brook, and also leased the Woolstans Wood estate where it finally reached the Severn. The plateway was constructed in 1796, at which time MacNab arrived in person to take charge of the works, replacing Anthony Gregson, the previous representative of the partners on the ground. MacNab built a large house for himself at Woolstans Wood and a much smaller one for his clerk. All was complete by January 1797, by which time large-scale coal production would have been possible. However, MacNab thought that he could see an additional business opportunity. There had recently been serious floods on the river Severn, resulting in demand for stone with which to rebuild bridges. There was building stone available at Woolstans Wood and the Billingsley Partners successfully tendered to supply stone for the rebuilding of Bewdley Bridge under the direction of Thomas Telford. Unfortunately, MacNab failed to inform the lessors of Woolstans Wood (Christchurch College, Oxford) about the quarry, and there is every likelihood that his intention was to defraud his landlords. Although Christchurch was eventually placated, more serious problems were looming for Messrs Johnson & Co[4].

The first sign of the impending crisis was in 1799, when the partners were forced to mortgage the Scotts estate and their interest in Woolstans Wood. Money was obviously running out. Two hundred years later it is possible only to guess at the sources of the problems, but there are a number of possibilities. The colliery adjoined old workings on the west at Southall Bank; as they would have been flooded and the new mine was to the dip of these, water was likely to have been a problem. Further to the north and east were a series of faults; mining has never been easy at Billingsley. There are also grounds for suspecting that Macnab's methods of management would not pass close inspection. Whatever the reason, Johnson & Co. were soon in serious trouble. The majority of the original partners had left, to be replaced by Thomas Telford, who was to regret his involvement at Billingsley. The mortgage provided only temporary relief and within a year there was another scheme to generate more income. This time an agreement was reached with Messrs Pemberton & Stokes, ironmasters of Oldswinford, for the latter to construct two blast furnaces at Billingsley. In return for generous terms on coal and ironstone, Pemberton & Stokes agreed to provide a loan to Johnson & Co. Although Pemberton & Stokes started work on the furnaces, they soon fell out with Johnson & Co. and the loan was never paid. There were two final blows. Firstly, George Johnson died while visiting the works at Billingsley to negotiate with Pemberton & Stokes. Secondly, some months later, MacNab fled to France, taking with him the books of the partnership and thereby explaining at least one reason as to why the mine had been losing money. With debts in excess of £10,000 the creditors moved in to take control of the company. Telford avoided the threat of bankruptcy as a co-partner in the scheme only because he was in Scotland and outside the jurisdiction of the English courts.

Having taken control of the affairs of the Billingsley company, the creditors agreed with the remaining partners to waive further bankruptcy proceedings provided their debts could be met by selling the mine. In 1802 it was sold by public auction to William Hazeldine, ironmaster of Shrewsbury and Bersham and colleague of Telford. This auction was enlivened by the presence of Childe's agent, who publicly declared that because Johnson & Co. had defaulted on their way-leave agreement (i.e. the agreement to allow the tramway over Childe's land), Childe now considered it void. This did not deter Hazeldine, probably because he was acting simply as an agent for a consortium made up of Thomas Rigby, former manager for Lord Stafford at his Lilleshall coal works, John Morris, a lawyer and Thomas Leek, a landowner. A fourth member of the consortium dropped out almost as soon as Hazeldine had made the purchase. Hazeldine paid the deposit on the purchase, and then handed matters over to Morris, Rigby and Leek. It might have seemed that the problems at Billingsley were about to be resolved. Sadly, this was far from the truth.

Rigby, Morris and Leek took possession of the works without paying the balance of the purchase price. This was allegedly done by Thomas Rigby using forged papers, who then dismissed the former workmen and replaced them with his own men. When challenged about the legality of his action, he is reported to have suggested he would never give up the works unless confronted with 'a file of soldiers'. The new occupiers of Billingsley were in fact very concerned about the leases negotiated by Johnson & Co. Some of the way-leaves were for less than the lease on the mine and Pulteney himself was only entitled to the Billingsley estates for his life. As he was an old man, this was of some importance. Pemberton & Stokes had now joined Childe in refusing to honour their agreements. Inevitably, the whole concern was halted for about two years while multiple cases were fought in chancery. It was not until 1805 that Rigby, Morris and Leek finally completed the sale and full production could begin again. By this time there had been some changes in personnel; Pemberton & Stokes had simply become Messrs Stokes, and this in turn was well on its way to being represented only by one man, George. He was putting together an impressive empire that included mines at Dudley & Sedgley, a rolling mill at Kinver, a forge at Eardington and a palatial house with grounds at Oldswinford, as well as much property in Kinver. The construction of the blast furnace at Billingsley completed the integration of his iron-working interests. In 1810 he purchased the mines at Billingsley from Rigby, Morris and Leake, as well as entering into a partnership with John Read, another iron-master and mine owner from Dudley. All this expansion came about on the back of an iron trade worked into frenzy by the demands of the Napoleonic Wars. Unfortunately, the next year brought a slump in the industry, and Stokes and Read both went bankrupt in mid-1812. Stokes's debts were estimated at £38,000. How long the works at Billingsley continued is unclear; probably the blast furnace closed immediately. It failed to sell as a going concern in 1814, and was then dismantled and sold as parts in 1817. The engines from the colliery were also sold at this time. At Scotts some working took place around the 1820s, in the areas left by previous generations; in Billingsley itself a little mining continued for a while, sustained by small-scale charter masters. However, there was to be no more large-scale investment in the area until the 1870s[5].

The various sales of the Billingsley works, with other sources, allow a picture to be built up of the equipment used. The 1801 sale mentions only a 38in pumping engine with 'machines', probably horse gins, for winding. There were a total of twenty-nine pits open, suggesting that the majority were probably rather small and shallow. Other items mentioned in the sale were shops for blacksmiths and carpenters and a counting house. By the time of the 1814 and 1817 dispersal sales the pumping engine had been joined by two whimseys (small steam engines) for winding, a small 'Trephetic' engine (a steam engine presumably designed by Richard Trevithick, pioneer of steam locomotion) with sliding rods, cranks and pumps and also a larger ungeared engine. There were still plenty of horse gins; two double gins and ten single gins. Smaller items included five flat pit ropes for winding, 120-200 yards long, forty-two railway wagons, thirty tons of iron rails with sleepers and 100 skips for use underground. At the blast furnace there was a 52in cylinder-blowing engine with two boilers, 640 tons of calcined iron, bar and round iron, and five tons of horseshoe moulds. The workings themselves passed through the sulphur coal to reach three seams of sweet coal (2ft to 4ft thick), at a total depth of 278ft. There was also ironstone, 20in to 28in thick, yielding 60% iron, and clay 'as good as Devon for pottery and crucibles'[6].

The failure of Billingsley in 1812 brought mining in this parish to a halt for almost half a century beyond some small-scale outcrop workings. However, in the 1860s a number of shafts and trials were put down. The exact sequence of events is no longer clear. However, it seems that two men, William Birchley of the Cape of Good Hope Inn in Billingsley and Edmund Breakwell were involved; perhaps sometimes working independently, sometimes together. By 1872 Birchley had started to sink for coal just to the east of the Cape of Good Hope, and in December he was able to report that he had struck a seam of sweet coal at 160 yards depth. With his brother Evan and a John Surtees, Birchley initially formed a partnership to work the colliery. However, it appeared that the colliery offered sufficient promise to warrant larger scale financing; press reports spoke of 13ft of coal, conveniently ignoring the fact that this was split into several seams, not all easily workable. The colliery was offered for sale in October 1874 and the old partnership was dissolved in 1875. The colliery was sold to one Samuel Taylor of Worcestershire in January 1875 and March that year saw the formation of the Billingsley Colliery Company with a share capital of £60,000. Taylor had made his money, somewhat implausibly, as a hairdresser and had gravitated towards becoming a stockbroker. The Birchley brothers and George Page (a Worcester solicitor who seems to have replaced Surtees) each got £5,000 of the new company's shares and directorships (the Birchleys, wisely, soon left the concern). The other key men in the concern were a group of Worcestershire businessmen and professionals, with John Thompson, a solicitor, apparently a driving force. William Mellor, a client of Thompson, was made chairman, with Thompson as manager. Thompson and Mellor enjoyed perhaps too close a financial relationship; Mellor had secured Thompson's professional services by promising to make him the sole beneficiary of his (Mellor's) will and also agreeing to loan the company £10,000 for construction of a railway line. Neither of these promises was ever carried out. The first managing director of the company was Thomas Pilditch, a Dorset civil engineer[7].

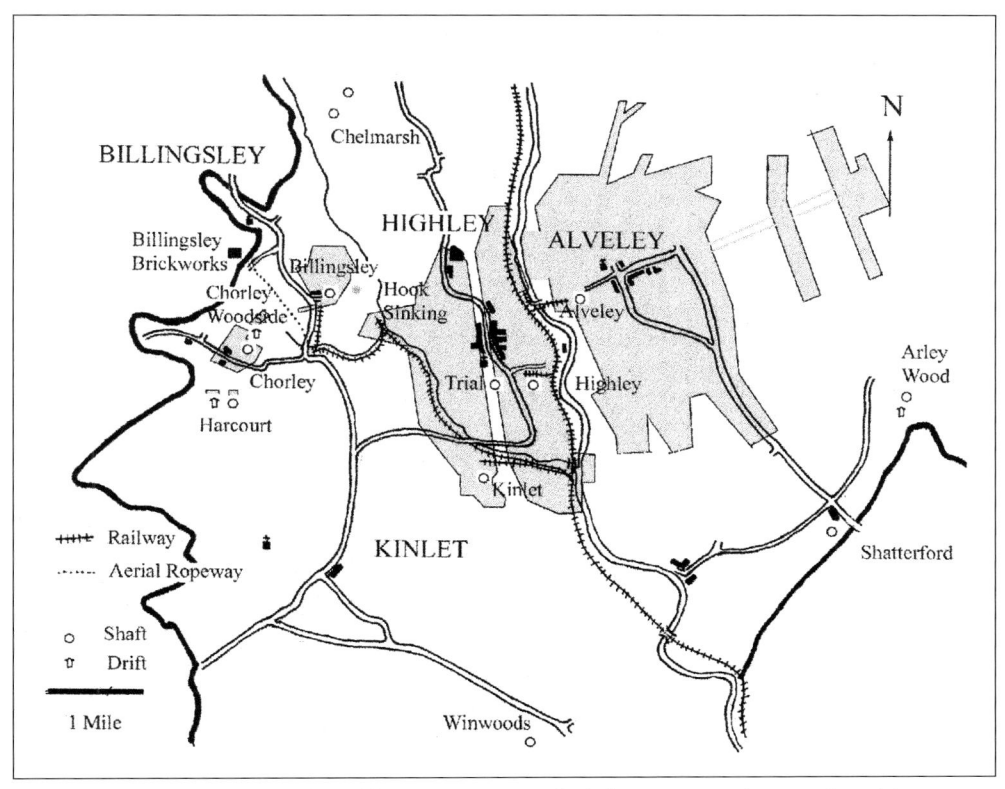

Mines of Billingsley and Highley, 1870-1970. Shaded areas are underground workings.

The priority of the company was to develop the mine and link it to the Severn Valley Railway. By 1877 a second shaft had been completed, and the workings were in two seams, with plans for an underground engine level heading north west. Extra mining leases were acquired to several hundred acres of land in Billingsley, and the route of the railway was plotted along the valley of the Borle Brook. Unfortunately, the completion of the second shaft was the only tangible achievement of the Billingsley Colliery Company and even that claimed the life of the banksman in an accident in 1876 that the inquest blamed on the mine manager. By 1878 the company owed Thompson £2,000, which could only be paid in shares, and in that year Samuel Taylor went bankrupt. Worse still, in January 1879 he was sentenced to eight months hard labour for fraud. His fellow directors must have been particularly embarrassed by the revelation that he had tried to settle some debts with its shares. Taylor's creditor showed shrewd judgement in rejecting these on the grounds the he 'had no faith in colliery shares'[8].

By the time Taylor's case came to court, the Billingsley Colliery Company had changed its appearance. In December 1878 the shareholders sold out to a Samuel Dimbleby, for £25,000, and soon afterwards the name was changed to the Severn Valley Colliery Company. However, some of the old hands remained, including Mellor and Thompson, with Thompson's partner, George Taylor, becoming secretary. Dimbleby must have found extra cash from somewhere, for on Monday 28 October 1879, the first sod of the railway was cut, in the presence of many invited guests and the press. Dimbleby was of the opinion that the reserves ran to fifty-one million tons of coal, free from gas and water. The contractors, Messrs Drew and Pickering, expected to complete the line by the end of January 1881. They did in fact seem to make rapid progress on the railway, but money to pay them was not forthcoming. Not surprisingly, work eventually stopped a mile short of the mine[9].

Mining at Billingsley seems to have been forever dogged by scandal and incompetence. A small, but illustrative, example of this was provided by the appearance in court of the junior clerk who worked in the company's Bridgnorth office. He had been quietly siphoning off receipts from coal sales into his own pocket. In true detective-book style, he was apprehended by the police on the deck of a ship in Liverpool, about to sail for America[10].

The failure to complete the railway was, of course, an altogether more serious matter, and led to Dimbleby floating another company, the Severn Valley Minerals Company, to take over proceedings, with £160,000 capital. This was to construct the railway link as well as a second colliery and the prospectus was laced with optimistic statements as to the value of the concern, attributed to eminent mining engineers. Unfortunately for Dimbleby, two of those eminent mining engineers, Henry Johnson and David Peacock, actually read the prospectus. Peacock commented that it contained 'a portion of a paragraph intended to mislead the public and in another part stated what was wholly untrue'. Dimbleby eventually withdrew their comments, but did so without any grace. Henry Johnson complained 'Mr Dimbleby called.... and was quite saucy'. Dimbleby reaped an appropriate reward with the failure of the flotation. Undaunted, he tried again in 1882 with the Severn Valley Coal, Iron and Clay Company, which was inflated both in name and share capital, now set at £200,000. Perhaps not surprisingly, it suffered the same fate as its predecessor. All these companies had at their centre Thompson and Mellor, as well as Dimbleby. The failure of this concern finally blew apart this partnership, with Thompson and George Taylor opposing the winding-up order on the Severn Valley Colliery Company sought by Dimbleby, and Mellor and Thompson filing cross-petitions against each other. Thompson *v.* Mellor was a particularly colourful action for slander[11].

Out of the legal morass, one figure emerged as a winner. Alfred Gibbs had started work for the Billingsley Colliery Company shortly after its formation in 1875 and was chief clerk. He was one of the main parties in the winding-up order, being owed £106, presumably in wages. Although he apparently had no background in mining before coming to Billingsley, he was both honest and a good businessman; qualities at a premium among mining entrepreneurs. By the end of 1882, he had purchased the mine. With the recent closure of Harcourt, and the run-down of mining on the Clee Hills, Billingsley was in a good position to serve a large tract of land in the hinterland of Bridgnorth and

Billingsley Colliery, c.1910. The original surface layout. On the left, the gentleman with the whiskers is George Tolley, the undermanager. On the right, by the office, are probably members of the Gibbs family who owned the pit.

Cleobury Mortimer. Under Gibbs's guidance, the colliery did this effectively for the next thirty years, working as a small landsale mine employing no more than thirty men, with an output of 5-6,000 tons per annum. Gibbs did very well from this, living next door to the mine at Prospect Farm and eventually becoming chairman of Bridgnorth District Council and a JP. For those men who preferred the traditional small-scale mine of the Wyre Forest Coalfield, Billingsley was a welcome refuge. The undermanager, George Tolley, had been the last man up from Harcourt. Another miner, George Robinson, a Lancastrian by birth, was a veteran of Eardington Colliery[12].

Although Billingsley brought little but trouble to its shareholders, it was significant in refocusing attention on the sweet coal of the Wyre Forest. In Highley a number of small mines had worked patches of sulphur coal since the failure of Stanley in the 1820s, but it was in the 1870s that the industry returned in style to the village. From the middle of the decade a group of North Staffordshire mine owners, chiefly members of the Viggars and Lawton families from Silverdale, began to show an interest in the area. In the grounds of a brickyard, two trial shafts were sunk to the sulphur coal. Using this experience, it was decided to sink production shafts just to the west of the old Stanley colliery and the railway station. In November 1877, the Highley Mining Company was formed to replace their previous partnerships, and in January 1878, work began on a pair of 9ft diameter shafts. The operation turned out to be something of a test of nerves, with firstly water to contend with and then the realization that the coal was much deeper than anticipated. Although

The pit top at Highley at the turn of the century. The original wooden headgear is present. The right-hand shaft was the first to be sunk; the 'old pit' was the downcast and coal-winding shaft. The machine on the right of the picture is a mortar mill driven by a steam engine. (Mrs Milburn).

the old Stanley seam was found, it was not possible to market this effectively and there was no prospect of the company earning any income until the sweet coal was reached. In December 1878 the manager reported that he daily expected to find this; by February of the next year both he and the sinkers had been dismissed. Finally, on 9 April 1879 the sweet coal was struck. The wait was worthwhile, for it was of good quality and thickness and was to be the foundation of the Highley Mining Company's prosperity. Unlike at Billingsley, the geology at Highley was not so formidable, with fewer faults and washouts of the seam. Nonetheless, the early years were still uncertain. It took another twelve months to finish the second shaft and get the mine in a state to produce coal. There was then an argument with the lessor, John Bradley-Beddard, as to the royalties that were to be paid, with the company arguing for a reduction from the original agreement. This culminated in a six-week shut down of the mine before an agreement was reached. There were also further changes of contractors and managers[13].

In spite of these early problems, the good quality of the coal and the proximity to the Severn Valley Railway ensured that the mine was a success. Following the opening of a temporary wharf at Highley Station, the pit-head was connected directly to the main line via a rope-worked incline in 1883, allowing rapid movement of coal in bulk to Bridgnorth, Kidderminster, Worcester and beyond.

A Highley Mining Company coal wagon. This photograph hung for many years in the offices of the company. (T.H. Stonehouse).

In 1883, a total dividend of 14.25% was paid and the company's capital was increased to £20,000. This was to set the direction for the future. Negotiations were started to secure the mineral rights on the surrounding properties and in June 1885 agreement was reached with the Kinlet Estate of William Lacon Childe to bore for coal[14]. It was to be some years before the Kinlet venture was translated into serious action. Possibly this was due to a downturn in the economy at the time. However, a borehole was put down, and as a result of this a new sinking began in 1892, close to Tippers Farm in Kinlet. This site had no road access, and so the mining leases also made provision for a railway from the Severn Valley running alongside the earthworks of the uncompleted Billingsley Colliery railway. Coal was struck in December 1893, at a depth of 296 yards, and the hooter at the works was sounded for forty minutes in celebration. In January the celebrations took a more practical turn when the entire workforce were taken by train for a meal at the Agricultural Hall in Bridgnorth. In a typical display of exuberance, speakers expressed the hope that that the whole district would soon become another North Staffordshire, covered with coal mines and houses, with Highley at the centre. The expectations of prosperity for the Highley Mining Company were perhaps more realistic[15].

Kinlet Colliery c.1915. The railway wagons were brought up the private mineral line from the Severn Valley branch to be loaded at the screens on the left of the photograph. The wooden headgear stands over the 16' diameter coal winding shaft. The cage and lifting chain can be seen. The photograph was taken in front of the locomotive shed to the north of the pit yard.

Kinlet Colliery c.1915. The small winding wheel on the left of the photograph carried the cage in the upcast shaft, known as the back pit. This was the ventilation shaft. The slightly taller building next to this is the open-topped fan housing and the gabled building with the door and arched windows is the steam operated fan house. The four Lancashire boilers are in the well between the chimney and the winding house. (Mrs M. Price).

In fact, Kinlet Colliery was something of a disappointment. Production started in the late 1890s, with the completion of the railway. The mine had a lavish 16ft diameter production shaft, claimed with some reason to be the best in the West Midlands, and a huge engine house and steam winder. There were hopes of finding additional seams below the Brooch. However, in spite of borings, these seams never materialized. What was found was basalt; a thick layer resulting from an old lava flow which had burnt out the coal where it came into contact with it and which formed a hard rock mass difficult to cut through and destructive of the colliery screens. The problems may have been behind an experiment in 1901 to try and make better use of the small coal and slack by compressing this into briquettes; (i.e. making large lumps of coal). This does not seem to have been particularly successful. Conditions did eventually improve to the north of the shafts, but working Kinlet was never easy[16]. However, it grew from employing about 150 men at the turn of the century to twice that by the start of the First World War, with an output of about 50,000 tons per annum. Highley was somewhat larger, with a 180-strong workforce more than doubling to almost 400

The brand-new locomotive Kinlet *at the works of Andrew Barclay, Kilmarnock, awaiting delivery to the Highley Mining Company's private mineral line to Kinlet colliery, 1896. On closure of the colliery the engine was sold to H.S. Pitt & Co., Pensnett, and named* Peter; *the pet name of the son of one of the directors. It is now in retirement at the Ironbridge Gorge Museum. (From GD329 in the Andrew Barclay Collection. Reproduced courtesy of the Keeper of the Records of Scotland & Glasgow University Archives & Business Records Centre).*

in 1914, and with output of about 75,000 tons per annum. The combined efforts of the two mines ensured that average dividends were usually over 20% for the company shareholders in the pre-war years[17].

While Highley and Kinlet grew, Billingsley stagnated. It remained a small mine for the first years of this century, and it must have been increasingly difficult for it to cope with its giant neighbours to the south. However, Alfred Gibbs, its owner, could not have lost sight of all of its former potential and, with the development of the Cleobury Mortimer and Ditton Priors Light Railway (CMDPLR) after 1901, he saw the chance of a rail connection and expansion. In 1907 plans were published for the Stottesdon, Kinlet and Billingsley Light Railway, to connect the colliery with the CMDPLR at Stottesdon. Whether Gibbs had any financial backers at this stage is unclear, but the plans were approved, with William Foxlee, engineer and director of the CMDPLR, to oversee the works. Nothing immediately materialized, but in July 1910 the Billingsley Colliery Company was registered. This was an ambitious project, but unlike its ill-starred predecessors thirty years earlier, its directors did include some men of proven ability. Most notable of these were the chairman, Sir Joseph Shaw, KC and Edmund Hann. They were also chairman and managing director of the mighty Powell-Duffryn Company, a giant in the South Wales Coalfield. The South Wales connection was also reflected by the inclusion of three other directors; H.T. Bailey (the secretary), James Strain and John Glasbrook, partners with Shaw in the Bedwas Colliery Company. All had other mining interests. Other directors included Gibbs, Foxlee, and William Childe of Kinlet Hall. On paper it looked a formidable combination. The company seems to have had no problem with their initial £75,000 share issue, or in acquiring mineral leases on the surrounding properties that the Highley Mining Company had not previously secured. The prospectus spoke optimistically of a mine producing 100,000 tons for twenty years, free from gas and water[18].

The new Billingsley Colliery Company saw that it had three major tasks ahead if it were to transform its mine. Firstly, there had to be a major reconstruction of the colliery, both on the surface and underground. Secondly, a railway was needed to take the coal away to the markets. Thirdly, houses were needed for the new workers at the mine. The reconstruction at the colliery was the easiest of these three tasks. The old surface arrangement consisted of winding-house, blacksmith's shop and office. The office was greatly expanded, while the other two were completely replaced and joined by a fan-house, carpenters and fitters shops, lamp room, garage and powerhouse. The latter housed the generators used to produce electricity for use both on the surface and down the mine. Underground a series of electric motors were installed on the main haulage roads to bring the coal to the pit bottom. The coal was obtained from four distinct seams and, perhaps for the first time in the coalfield, use was made of a coal cutter[19].

The first plan for a rail link to the mine was via the prospective Stottesdon, Kinlet and Billingsley Light Railway and so to Cleobury Mortimer and the Great Western

Billingsley Colliery, c.1914. Alf Jones, the engineman, stands by the Thornwill and Wareham winding engine in the newly built winding house. Both shafts were served by the winder. (L. Jones).

line from Bewdley to Wooferton. When this project failed, the alternative of following the route of the 1880 Billingsley Railway was decided upon. This had the advantage that many of the earthworks were already in place. A different alignment was used to reach the colliery itself; rather than follow the Borle Brook all the way, a tributary was followed to a place called Priors Moor, about half a mile and 300ft below the mine. At this point the screens for the mine were constructed. They were connected to the pithead by means of a rope-worked narrow gauge tramway. Extensive engineering works were needed at Priors Moor to divert a brook to allow construction of the buildings and trackwork. There was a long-term aim to extend the railway further north alongside the Borle Brook to reach a new sinking at Hook Coppice[20].

Billingsley screens and sidings, c.1915. Local photographer Reg Southern published this picture as a postcard in 1916. The Billingsley branch line terminated at this point. Coal came down the incline from the colliery in tubs to be screened and loaded into railway wagons. Materials and waste from the screens were sent back up with the empty tubs. The aerial ropeway from Billingsley Brickworks also terminated here. Tiles, bricks and clay ware came down from the brickworks for loading into railway wagons. Coal for the kilns was sent back to the brickworks. The screens and aerial ropeway were driven by electric motors powered by a steam generator at the colliery.

The company did construct some 'temporary' prefabricated sheet-iron bungalows next to the colliery site at Billingsley. However, it decided to build most of its houses at the north end of Highley, giving the workers better access to the facilities of the growing village, at the price of a two mile walk to the mine involving a steep hill in both directions. The first houses to be built in 1912 formed a rather grim brick terrace, but plans were afoot for a 200-house garden village, funded by the nominally independent Woodhill Garden Village Co. Ltd. These houses were much better than anything else available in the village at that date, with mains water and sewerage[21].

Serious development work started in 1911; in September of that year Messrs Caffin and Co., railway contractors, started work on the railway. There were problems with landslips along the route, exacerbated by exceptionally wet weather. The village also paid host to a collection of hard-drinking navvies, memories of whom lived on for many years. At New England, Caffin & Co. opened a stone quarry, one of the last to be at work in a district once noted for its stone. The railway was eventually approved as suitable for traffic in April 1913. It had cost well over £30,000[22].

The year 1912 was not a good one for the Billingsley Colliery Company. While Caffin's steam navvy was sinking into the mud, problems were multiplying on other fronts. In January, a miner called Thomas Homer was asphyxiated underground when an air pipe was fractured. The resulting inquest revealed very lax management, with the company employing two deputies to supervise work that needed three. In March work was halted for three weeks by the national coal strike. In July Alfred Gibbs, the mentor of the mine, died. There then began a series of disputes with the rural district council over the new houses that were to dog the company for the rest of its life. The bungalows at Billingsley were condemned as unsanitary and haulage of materials between the company's brickworks in Billingsley and the building sites in Highley caused so much damage to the roads that in 1914 the district council sued the company for damage done to the highway. The Billingsley Colliery Company won the latter case, but not before it had been forced to build an aerial ropeway from the brickyard to the railhead at Priors Moor to ease road haulage, and had alienated the local councils[23].

The following year, 1913, brought little change in the company's fortunes. The railway was completed and preliminary work began at the site of the new sinking

Pit top at Billingsley Colliery, c.1916. The right-hand No.2 shaft was the coal winding shaft. Shaft No.1 on the left was the upcast. Return air drawn up this shaft by the steam driven fan escaped through the flat-topped chimney to the right of the headframe.

The rescue team at Billingsley Colliery, 1920. Standing in front of the ambulance are, from left to right, F. Peake (surveyor), E. Pountney, -?-, N. Askey, Bill Foster; sitting; Jim Whittle, Alf Westwood, Harry Price. (Mrs G. Foster).

in Hook Coppice. However, there was fresh humiliation in the courts at the hands of the local Miners Federation, who successfully sued for breach of contract on behalf of three of their members who had been dismissed from the company. Work began on the new Garden Village and was almost immediately halted by a strike of the labourers. More damaging was another row with the district council, this time over the sewerage scheme for the project. When the first of the houses were ready in 1914, the council initially refused to grant them occupation licenses. The company at this stage doubled its capital to £150,000 and also took out a £16,000 mortgage to try and raise more cash. By the summer of 1914 the company had somehow managed to employ 200 men, in spite of the housing problem, and the mine was in production. Then came the First World War. Within four months of the outbreak of hostilities, 60% of the underground workers had left the mine for the armed forces (an eloquent comment on both local patriotic fervour and conditions at Billingsley). Weekly output, planned to be several thousand tons, was actually 800 tons. Work on the new sinking was abandoned and the company recruited a number of Belgian miners displaced by the German invasion of their country. This was all in vain. Capital was increased still further, to £180,000 in 1915, but the situation did not improve. In the summer of that year, the directors considered wholesale closure, but this was avoided by an offer of purchase from the Highley Mining Company. This went ahead in September 1915[24].

The real motives of the Highley Mining Company in purchasing Billingsley were probably complex. They certainly obtained a going colliery, and perhaps they really did believe that they could make it profitable. However, Billingsley had extensive mineral leases, extending into the north of Highley, and these also formed part of the purchase. By buying the company they made sure that they controlled all the reserves of coal in the vicinity, and ensured that they would never again face a serious local rival. In the event they seem to have achieved rather little at Billingsley itself. The most fundamental problem lay with the geology, as the coal was cut off by old workings or faults on nearly three sides. The best coal was found down a one in three gradient in an area known as the 'water hole', a name that speaks volumes about underground conditions. The colliery continued to operate until 1921, but with an output still around 800 tons per week. In the summer of that year there was a long national miners strike. At this point, the company decided that it could no longer afford to continue with Billingsley and it was closed in September. The pick of the machinery was transferred to Highley or Kinlet, where a significant number of men also soon found work. The buildings at Billingsley were left empty, eventually finding use as a farmyard. The occupants of the cottages next to the mine, in addition to losing their jobs, also lost their electricity supply, which had been generated at the colliery. The reserves in the north of Highley were eventually entered in the 1930s from Kinlet and Highley Collieries[25].

Despite the problems inherited from Billingsley and the difficulties inevitably caused by the First World War, the Highley Mining Company entered the 1920s

Highley pit top, 1916. The winding house is in the centre of the picture with the brick chimney enveloped in steam. The low circular chimney on the right may be the exhaust from the 'new pit'. This shaft carried air out of the pit and at one time relied on a furnace to achieve a current of air.

The wooden headgears at Highley Colliery in 1916. The newly-erected coal screening plant on the left-hand side of the photograph straddles the standard gauge rails of the wagon incline connected to the Severn Valley branch line. Empty coal wagons were drawn up the incline by a rope attached to the descending loaded wagons. The wagons were manoeuvred at the top of the incline using heavy horses and later by a steam driven haulage engine.

in fundamentally good shape[26]. Labour relations and the post-war depression were major challenges for the coal industry nationally in the 1920s. At Highley these were not as serious as they might have been. The company was badly hit by a national strike in 1921, but not as badly as the local Miners Federation, which effectively collapsed at the end of the dispute (see Chapter 2). Thus in the General Strike of 1926 there was only a short stoppage. The post-war depression particularly hit producers of coal for export and industrial markets; Highley and Kinlet chiefly produced household coal and their markets were not so badly affected.

A sign that the Highley Mining Company was optimistic about the future came with the introduction of electricity at Highley and Kinlet, leading to increased mechanization.[27] This was introduced in 1916 as part of a larger renovation scheme, perhaps with the company benefiting from experience gained at Billingsley. Power was generated at Highley and taken by underground cable to Kinlet. The company also introduced a coal cutter at Highley, a Hopkinson chain cutter. By 1921 experiments with electric motors to drive the haulage system were being carried out on the south side of the pit, and these were the cause of a fatal accident in that year. When Billingsley closed, the company was eventually able to entice the chief engineer, William Foster, to take over at Highley and he continued

The first coal-cutting machine at Highley Colliery, 1916. In charge of the Hopkinson coal cutter is Fred Beddoe. (T.H. Stonehouse).

The steam winding engine at Kinlet Colliery c.1915. Despite exhaustive enquiries the details of this engine remain a mystery. Folklore tells us that it was a converted marine engine, although judging by its size this seems unlikely. (Mrs M. Price).

Kinlet Colliery back pit winding engine, c.1915. Again the history of this engine is obscure except that it originally drove a flat winding rope. This rope was replaced by a circular rope but the original winding drum was retained. Riding in the shaft could be an alarming experience as the rope would flip off its coils as the drum rotated, giving a jerky ride. The lad in this picture is Tom Cadwallader who later worked in the offices at Highley, becoming the office manager at Alveley. (Mrs M. Price).

An aerial view of Highley Colliery, c.1935, taken in midsummer. Note the stacks of coal. In order to maintain full production in the summer months, coal was stacked ready for the autumn sales. In the background is Highley Station.

the modernization scheme, both on the surface and underground. By 1930 the majority of coal was being cut by machine and much of the haulage relied on electric motors.[28] At Kinlet progress was slower and experiments with coal cutters ended in failure, although some success was had with a Siskol heading machine. However, hand coal getting was to remain almost universal at the pit. Haulage also depended very largely on a continuous rope system driven from the surface or on self-acting inclines; the jigs. Some use was made of electric motors in the newer workings. More progress was made on the surface with the replacement of the original wooden headgears with steel, a new main winding engine and also a new engine house for the small shaft.[29]

Towards the end of the 1920s the Highley Mining Company started to consider how best to exploit new reserves in the area. A number of options were considered. Plans were drawn up for a new colliery to the west of the existing Kinlet shafts, linked to it by an extension of the railway. This was particularly favoured by one of the directors, Harry Eardley. With his death in 1933 the scheme lost its chief proponent and continued concerns about the extent of underground basalt also weighed against it. Serious consideration was also given for a while to a sinking close to Hampton Loade, but here the extent of the coal was largely unknown.[30] In 1930, for the first time workings from Highley crossed under the river to Alveley, where the coal continued to be of high quality. Ultimately, it was decided that the future for the company lay with a new sinking in Alveley. A production shaft here would be adjacent to new reserves of proven quality and furthermore the new mine could be laid out according to modern principles. Thus it was in 1935 that the first sod of the new Alveley Colliery was cut in a highly publicized ceremony.[31]

There had been some debate as to the exact form of the new Alveley Colliery; at one stage there was talk of using a drift to reach the coal. This was rejected but the colliery was unconventional in that it only had a single, 365-yard deep shaft. This was possible because the workings were simply an extension of those of the Highley Colliery, with good underground communication between the two. The Highley shafts were retained for ventilation and for emergency access underground. While it may not have been the original intention to make this a permanent arrangement, it was found that it worked well and a second shaft was never added at Alveley.[32] Although money was saved by this measure, in other respects it was lavished on the project to ensure that the mine was as efficient as possible. The headframe was constructed of futuristic ferro-concrete, and electric winding was used. Steam was completely banished by electricity and the pit top was landscaped and even provided employment for gardeners. Underground, conveyors progressively replaced pit ponies in moving the coal off the face to the main haulage. Coal cutters were universal. To move the coal from the pit to the markets, a new set of screens were constructed on the Severn Valley Railway and linked to the pit by an endless rope system. This crossed the Severn on a new concrete bridge. All coal and man haulage had been transferred from Highley to Alveley by September 1940.[33] Kinlet had previously been abandoned in

Work starts on the sinking of Alveley shaft, 1936. The winding house and reinforced concrete headgears were constructed before work started on the shaft. This allowed the sinking to be carried out using the original headframe. The winding engine used for the sinking was replaced by the Metropolitan Vickers winder on completion of the sinking.

The reinforced concrete headgear under construction in 1935.

September 1937, when the leases on the Kinlet Estate expired. The mine had proved impossible to mechanize and there were continued problems with basalt having burnt out the coal (ironically, at the time of closure, workings entered some of the best ground ever encountered at the mine). The loss of Kinlet actually mattered very little to the company; in 1935 the output from Kinlet and Highley combined was 200,000 tons per annum; by 1945 Alveley was producing almost 250,000 tons each year.[34]

Alveley colliery was a sound investment. With wartime conditions progress was slower than the company might have liked, but towards the end of the conflict targets were regularly exceeded and production records broken. Unfortunately for the Highley Mining Company, there was to be no peacetime dividend as the elections in 1945 brought about a Labour Government committed to nationalization of the mines. Unlike their counterparts in Bayton (see below), the Highley Mining Company recognized the inevitable and settled instead to get the best possible compensation for their prize asset (a matter not helped by

The endless rope haulage tub tramway in 1937. The tramway connected the pit top to the screens 1,100 yards away alongside the Severn Valley branch of the Great Western Railway. In the middle distance can be seen the abutments of the new bridge. On the horizon are the Working Men's Club and the gable ends of the terraced streets of Highley. (T.H. Stonehouse).

Constructing the tramway from the bridge to the screens in 1937. In the background is Potter's Loade cottage. (T.H. Stonehouse).

The railway embankment was extended in width to accommodate the tramway. Material came from the spoil tip at Kinlet with ash from Buildwas and Stourport power stations. The material was spread and consolidated by manual labour. Nearly all the men involved in the work were employed by the Highley Mining Company, brought out of the pit for the summer months.

Shaft sinkers at Alveley pit top, August 1936. The shaft lies under the boarded platform on which they are standing. The winding kibble is suspended above their heads. At the bottom right on the steps lies the first lump of coal to come out of the mine from the Brooch seam.

Sinking Alveley shaft in 1936. The shaft was 15 feet in diameter and 340 yards deep. The sinkers are hand-loading the kibble to be lifted to the surface.

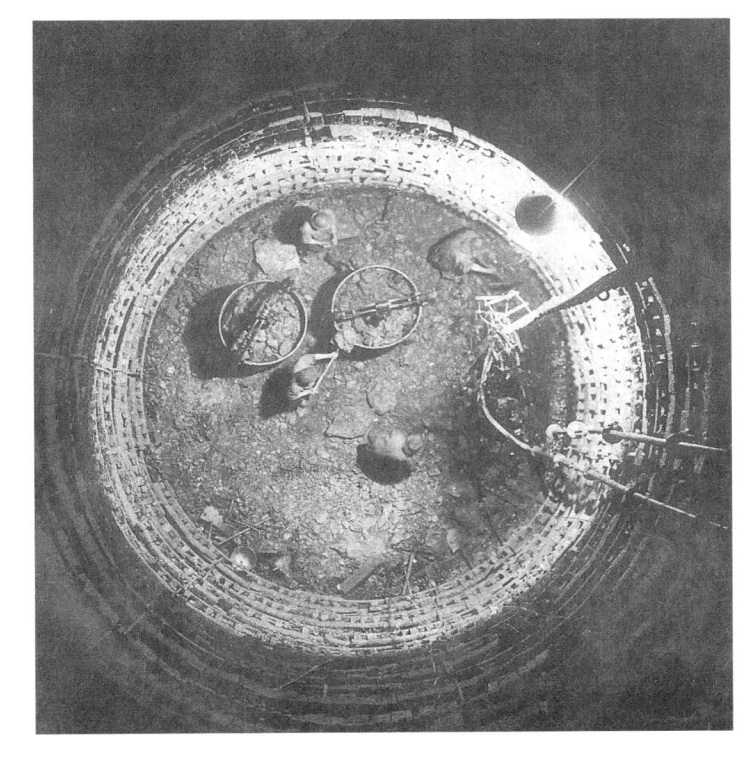

the ownership of a large quantity of houses considered by the NCB to be a liability). As in many similar concerns, the miners generally welcomed nationalization, and vesting day in 1947 was marked by a short ceremony involving the two oldest surface and underground men. Again, entirely typical, there was little immediate change at the pit, although the manager, Sam Machin, was soon promoted and replaced by the then youngest manager in the country, Ray Hasbury.[35]

The Coal Board maintained steady investment in Alveley, completely phasing out pit ponies in favour of face conveyors, although retaining the old system of rope haulage on the main trunk roads to the shaft. In some ways, coal getting remained rather traditional, with the roads closely following the contours of the seams and loading of the conveyors all done by hand. Electrification was extended to the winding engine and fan at Highley. At Alveley, pit head baths arrived in 1950 and a coal washery was erected. Output gradually crept up to 300,000 tons per annum in 1957, with employment at just over 1,000 men.[36]

By 1954 the NCB began to plan the future for Alveley. The workings were advancing eastwards to a major fault, the Romsley Fault. To ascertain the condition of the coal beyond that, a series of boreholes were put down. These demonstrated that the Brooch was thrown down almost 50 yards but its thickness and quality remained good. They also proved the presence of the Staffordshire Thick Coal, apparently in workable condition, thus finally realizing the dreams of a score of Victorian speculators. In total, there were estimated to be something like 50 million tons of coal present, enough to give the mine a life of fifty years. To get the new coal, a number of options were possible, including sinking a completely new set of shafts beyond the fault. Eventually, it was decided to get the coal from Alveley by means of a new horizontal road engineered to take railway locomotives and trains from the pit bottom to the coal face. Thus, the old systems of rope haulage were finally to be banished in favour of mine cars and horizon mining. To ensure a level gradient, the shaft at Alveley had to be deepened by 50 yards. The new main haulage road then ran straight for $2\frac{1}{2}$ miles, intersecting the old workings part way and piercing the Romsley Fault. It was then intended to intersect first the Brooch seam and eventually the thick coal beyond.[37]

Work on the New Development was formally authorized in 1958. The underground development continued at the same time as normal coal getting in the old workings. However, once the locomotive road was complete coal was sent onto this for transfer to the pit bottom and the old winding stage was abandoned. To ensure adequate ventilation to the new system, a shaft had to be sunk to connect the old workings with the new road, and during the construction of this two contractors were killed. Despite this, by the summer of 1960 the new arrangements were ready and they were commissioned over the August holiday. It was not until 1964 that all the workings were in the new area east of the Romsley Fault. At the same time as work was being undertaken underground, there was also extensive redevelopment on the surface. A new complex was constructed to house the medical and deployment centres, the canteen and

Banksman Tom Chad on the top deck at Alveley shaft top in 1954. The cage is fitted with removable gates for man-riding.

Tom Chad in 1964 after the reconstruction of Alveley. He is dwarfed by mine cars lined up to go down the shaft. (Shropshire Star).

Alveley pit top c.1958. The empty coal tubs have returned from their 1.25 mile round trip to the screens and washery and are about to be sent back underground for loading. The cage carried four 10cwt tubs at a time, two on each deck. Leaning on the handrail is oil man George Burgess. (H. Turner).

The aerial ropeway that replaced the tub tramway at Alveley in 1960. Constructed by Mitchell Ropeways of Doncaster, it was 1,100 yards long and carried coal from the shaft to the washery. (Mitchell Ropeways).

lamproom. The rope-worked tramway connecting the pit top with the screens was replaced with an aerial ropeway, also complete by 1960. The pit had received something like £1 million in new investment, and was forecast to have a secure future.[38]

Unfortunately for Alveley, the climate in which the coal industry was operating was changing very quickly. Throughout most of the 1950s, the country had been chronically short of coal, and the NCB's role was to mine this, almost irrespective of the price. Towards the end of the decade the demand for coal started to drop as more efficient use was made of the fuel and other energy sources became available. This was to set the scene for the 1960s and the NCB rapidly found itself producing more coal that it could sell. In this environment, Alveley was not in a good position. It was isolated from most markets and, following the closure of the railway northwards through Bridgnorth to Buildwas Power Station, it became absolutely dependent on Stourport Power Station to take its coal. With the rapid decrease in the demand for household coal, the Brooch lost much of its natural market. The colliery also had just one reliable seam, for the quality of the Staffordshire Thick Coal was unknown this far to the west. Significantly, production never reached the levels of most of the 1950s and output per man was

The angle station on the aerial ropeway. In the background are the telegraph poles of the railway. The angle station was subject to heavy stresses from the combined loads of the buckets and the suspended running rope. Over 1,000 cubic yards of concrete were poured into the excavation to counter this loading. (Mitchell Ropeways).

A view of the washery from the aerial ropeway pylons. Empty railway wagons are lined up for loading. On the right of the picture are the slurry settlement lagoons and the Severn. (Mitchell Ropeways).

poor compared to other mines in the West Midlands area. The fate of Alveley depended on further mechanization at the coal face to increase productivity.[39]

While the redevelopment had modernized most aspects of the mine, the actual process of coal getting was essentially unchanged from 1940, with coal cutters removing the coal from the seam, and loaders manually shovelling it onto the conveyors to begin its journey to the face. To bring output to an acceptable level, this had to be replaced by the technology of power-loading, where the whole operation was mechanized. The first power loaders were introduced in 1966 and initial results were good; in May 1967 the local press were shown round the mine and the pit was actively recruiting new workmen.[40] However, when the machines were moved to a new face, problems became apparent. A combination of faulting, a dirt band that got mixed up in the coal reducing its quality, and difficulties in keeping the roads open all made for an unhappy time. The area management became concerned in the summer of 1967 and in November warned that the mine was in danger of closure. In January 1968 it was announced that the pit was to close in June unless there were marked improvements. By February it was making a profit, but the NCB merely confirmed the date of closure. This provoked a furious local reaction and after much pressure the NCB relented.

However, to many it confirmed that the NCB were determined to close the pit

Inside the winding house at Alveley Colliery, 1967. At the controls is engineman Bill Amphlet. The winder was powered by a Metropolitan Vickers 750hp electric motor and could wind the cage carrying 2.5 tons of coal in 40 seconds.

Marie Price and Betty Webb (past and current colliery secretaries) inspect the last load of coal to come out of the pit at Alveley, Friday 24 January 1969.

regardless of the circumstances and that it was time to get out. Throughout the spring and summer the pit led a hand-to-mouth existence, with low morale and expectations. The next face to be selected for mechanization was widely considered to be one of the worst ever seen at the mine, and losses of £50,000 over July and August were unsurprising. The announcement of closure in December was equally anticipated, although the NCB's comments that this would not cause the men to have a bad Christmas were unappreciated. After an appeal, closure was in fact delayed to the end of January 1969 and salvage meant that final abandonment did not happen until March of that year. About fifty men transferred to other pits; either Granville near Lilleshall or Cannock Chase. Most were made redundant and eventually found work in light engineering or the carpet factories in Bridgnorth, Kidderminster and Telford. The area was expanding as overspill housing for the West Midlands, and this process continued unabated. By 1969, Highley was rapidly ceasing to be a mining village and, even if the colliery had survived, its impact would have naturally diminished.[41]

6

PENSAX, ABBERLEY AND ROCK

The first clear reference to coal mining in Pensax comes in 1565, when the Dean and Chapter of Worcester Cathedral leased a coal mine to the City of Worcester Corporation. Behind this move lay a local fuel crisis, due to the scarcity of firewood. The Corporation wished to secure an alternative fuel for their use. Interestingly, Shrewsbury Corporation embarked on a similar venture at about this time with a mine at Hanwood[1]. The Worcester venture continued until at least 1574, after which it vanishes from the Corporation accounts. Transport of coal to the city must have been a significant hurdle, for Pensax is some distance from a navigable river and this must have counted against the mine.

In the seventeenth century the Pensax mines can be traced through a series of leases made by the Dean and Chapter of Worcester. In 1610 one T. Vincent was authorized to get coal on the common and in 1617 a Mr Salloway paid 6s a ton for ironstone. The Bailiff of Pensax in 1634 was instructed to stop all mines on the common but was then allowed to sink for coal on the waste in 1642. In 1651 the Parliamentary Commissioners dismissed the coal in Menith Wood as not being worth the digging, but in 1668 Henry Tolley took out a lease[2].

In the early eighteenth century the Clutton family first appear as mine owners. Thomas Clutton obtained a twenty-one-year lease to coal under the land of Worcester Cathedral in 1724, on paying a royalty of 1s per ton. Their mines were developed on their Pensax Court estate, in the middle of the parish. In 1744 a neighbour was to describe these mines, on oath, as some of the most productive in the Kingdom. Doubtless this was an exaggeration, but the Cluttons were to do well financially from them for many years. They were not, however, an unmixed blessing; the heir to the family fortune was thrown down a mineshaft by his horse and killed in 1754. The mines were apparently worked directly by the Cluttons until about 1790 when they were leased to Samuel Bray. Bray also leased the farmland on the estate and the neighbouring Bough's Farm in Stockton, with an eye on its presumed coal. Although he held Pensax

Court until his death in 1810, the Cluttons did not repeat the experiment of leasing out the mines and placed the following advertisement in *Berrow's Worcester Journal*:

> Pensax Coal Works. The said coal works are now in the hands of the proprietor, and every exertion will be used for the accommodation of the public, the weight will be particularly attended to and the roads (which have been repaired) are now perfectly good.

It seems that at least during the latter period of Bray's stewardship, all was not well at Pensax Court. With the works back in the hands of the Clutton family, there was a long period of prosperity[6].

By the 1750s other mine owners in Pensax start to appear in the records; in 1759 the Revd Thomas King was exploiting the coal beneath his estate at Penn Hall[3]. In 1783 this was being worked by Robert Cooke, who also farmed the land and had a business as a tallow chandler, soap maker and grocer. Although the coals were to be got 'at an easy expense out of virtually every field', Cooke went bankrupt in 1785, and the colliery does not feature again until the mid-nineteenth century. North of Penn Hall is Stile House, and here in 1833 John Bray was operating a coal mine that had been in existence since at least 1808[5]. South of Penn Hall, at Woodhouse, the Knott family was working coal around 1790.

By 1800 virtually every estate in the parish had its own coal mine and a significant group of men earned their living as charter-masters, contracted to work these mines. Details are shown in Table 6.1. The most prominent of these were the Craddock family. They were living in Pensax in the seventeenth century, but it is not until the later eighteenth century that they are recorded as coal owners. In 1761, Richard Craddock leased mines in St Clairs Field on the Old Hall estate of the Browning family and in 1795 this was extended to nearby Wigmore Meadow. In 1797 there is a reference to the 'engine pit' of 'Mr Craddock', indicating that the works were of some size and sophistication. Adjacent to the Old Hall estate was the Far Town estate and here John, another member of the Craddock family, leased both the farm and colliery from at least 1783. John also operated a coal mine at Snead, just over the parish boundary in Rock. However, he went bankrupt in 1792 and Thomas Cole, a Kinlet man who had married into one of the local coal mining families in 1787, then worked Far Town Coal Works. Cole was still present at Far Town in 1807, but by 1840 the Craddocks were back as tenants[4].

In the south of the coalfield the years around the turn of the nineteenth century were dominated by the partial construction of the Leominster Canal. For the Pensax collieries, the failure to complete the canal deprived them of the chance to sell their coal to anything but the traditional local market. It is perhaps a moot point as to whether the completion of the canal to Stourport, thereby allowing Shropshire and South Staffordshire coal into the Wyre Forest's heartland, would have been to the advantage of any of the local mines; this point however, was

Table 6.1. Mining in Pensax and district, 1750-1850

Name	Details	References
Boughs Farm	Stockton parish	BWJ 23/4/07, 5/12/33, R. Baugh, Map of Worcs
Heath Farm	1807 Coal and ironstone advertised, 1844 coal advertised.	BWJ 3/9/07, 27/6/44
Woodhouse	1773 Coal advertised, 1786-90 John Knott owner, 1804 coal advertised.	BWJ 29/7/73, 5/10/86, 22/11/04
Penn Hall	1759 Rev King owner, 1772 Mrs King owner, 1783-5 Robert Cook owner, 1825 Coal advertised.	BWJ 17/5/59, 13/8/72, 27/3/83, 12/5/85, 6/12/25
Stile House	1807 Coal advertised as proved on the estate, 1808 Mine shown on map, 1833 John Bray owner	BWJ 23/4/07, 5/12/33, R. Baugh, Map of Worcs
Pensax Court	Owned throughout by Clutton family, 1792-1810 sublet to Sam Bray	See text
Old Hall	Owned Brown family: 1761-c.1804. sublet to Richard Craddock, 1805-6 Pensax Coal & Iron Company. Later amalgamated with Far Town.	See text
Far Town	1783 John Craddock tenant, 1797-1807 Thos Cole tenant, 1840 John Cole tenant	BWJ 27/3/83, 23/3/97, 26/11/07, 11/6/40
Snead and Hawkley	1772 Mine shown on map, 1797-c 1830 William Warren owner, 1828 coal advertised on the estate	I. Taylor, Map of Worcs., BWJ 23/3/97, R. Baugh, Map of Worcs., BWJ 26/12/28
Snead	1785-92 John Craddock	BWJ 5/5/85, 16/2/92
Stildon	1759 Richard Clutton, 1770 Coal mine advertised on estate	BWJ 15/5/59, 11/10/70

BWJ: Berrows Worcester Journal. Dates cover 1750-1850.

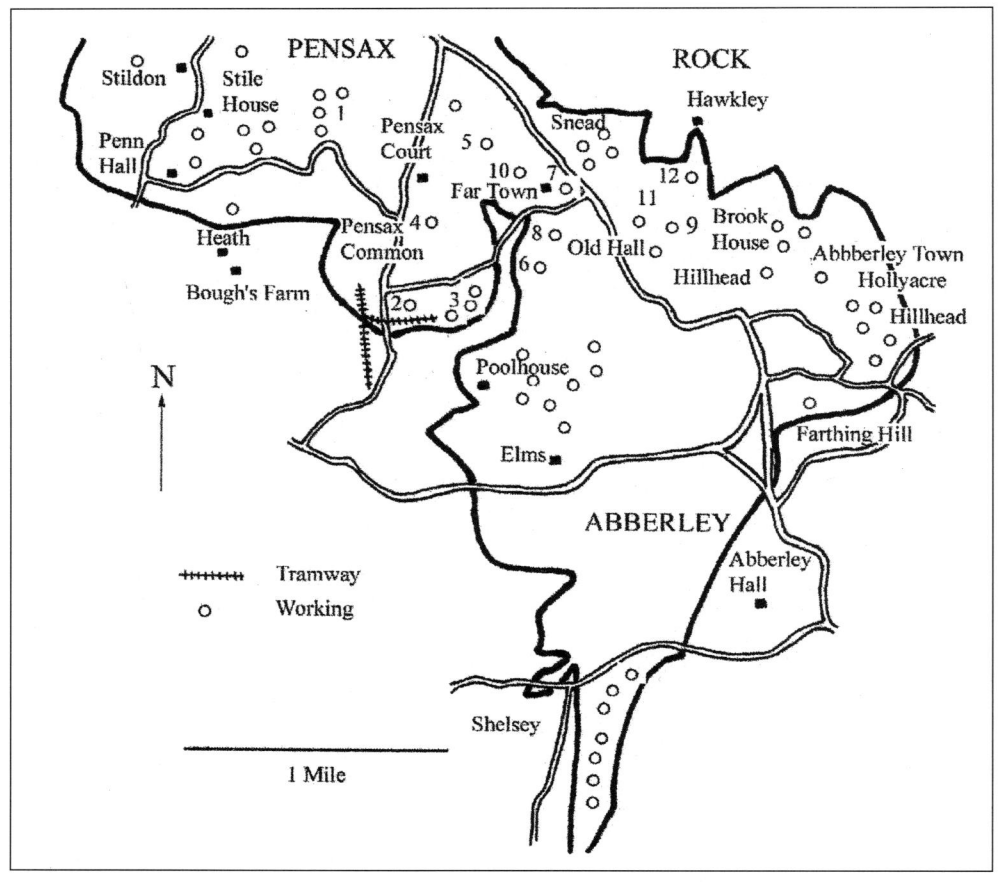

Mines of Pensax and Abberley c.1750-1850.

Details of individual shafts, where known: Pensax Court; 1. ?-1828, 2. 1772, 3. c.1828-1844, 4. c.1850-1855, 5. 1854-1860. Old Hall; 6. St Clairs 1761-1795, 7. Old Pit c.1790, 8. Townsfield 1792-c.1800, 9. Wigmore 1795-c.1830. Far Town; (10, 11, 12) c.1780-1840.

never considered by the Pensax coal owners. Instead they renewed their efforts to complete the construction of the waterway. This climaxed in 1805 with the promotion of the Pensax Coal and Iron Company. This optimistic venture centred on the Old Hall Estate of the Browning family, and involved the opening of new mines and the construction of a blast furnace to work an alleged seam of ironstone on the land. In turn, this would provide the impetus for the completion of the canal. The schemes were to be financed with £20,000 capital divided up as 100 equal shares. Little is known of the individuals behind the company; the chairman was Sir Christopher Smith, a local landowner, but others may have provided the real impetus. The venture was flawed from the start; regardless of the quality or quantity of ironstone still available, the sulphur coal would have been quite unsuitable to smelt it. The share-buying public was not moved by the prospectus; it is clear that by early 1806 there was a shortage of subscribers and the venture quietly faded away[7].

There were periodic attempts to complete the canal, either as a waterway or by a tramway, but none of these ever came to fruition. The Clutton-Brocks at Pensax Court eventually constructed tramways from some of their mines leading via a steep incline to Wharf House at Stockton. Here the coal must have been loaded onto carts for road haulage along the lower Teme valley. This apparently worked until about 1840[8].

By the middle of the nineteenth century, coal was being worked in Pensax at Far Town, Stile House, Penn Hall and Pensax Court (the last by Thomas Clutton-Brock). There was a slow retrenchment of the industry as existing mines were worked out, leaving only the Pensax Court mines. Even these were in some disarray. In the 1850s the Clutton-Brock holdings at Pensax Court started to disintegrate as the family estates were sold amid courtroom battles. Eventually in 1862 the estates and mines were purchased by James Higginbottom, a Bolton businessman. In this year four pits were worked; in 1866 there were three, producing about 3-4,000 tons of coal per annum. In December of that year the pit bottom at the main drainage shaft collapsed. Although there was no loss of life, it was not judged economic to reopen the mine and of the remaining pits, one was worked from a single shaft. However, in 1873 there was an abortive proposal to link the collieries to the Bewdley and Tenbury railway. Higginbottom himself was an acrimonious character who made numerous enemies, including Daniel Simmonds, his nephew and estate manager, and some at least of his workmen. This could not have helped the mines and in about 1876, Higginbottom closed them down. While there was a little mining subsequently on adjoining properties, this was the end of concerted activity[9].

To the south of Pensax, in Abberley, the Bury family have left extensive accounts dealing with their mines and other interests in the 1730s. They employed three contractors to get the coal, each in charge of a separate pit. They also worked the limestone on Abberley Hill, doubtless using the slack from the pits to burn this. On the larger estates it was common to work a colliery in conjunction with either lime or brickworks and this represents an early example of this practice[10]. Details of mining in the later eighteenth century are very sketchy, although matters become a little clearer at the start of the nineteenth century. Poolhouse colliery in the west of the parish (destined to become the largest mine in Abberley in the late nineteenth century) was operating by 1815. In the east of the parish Hollyacre Colliery was also destined for a long life and is first recorded in 1821. The surrounding estates also seem to have had coal mines; once owned by a Thomas Griffiths, which must have been close to Hollyacre, there was a steam engine present in 1825[11]. By the middle of the century William Norwood, possibly with other unrecorded charter-masters, was busy at

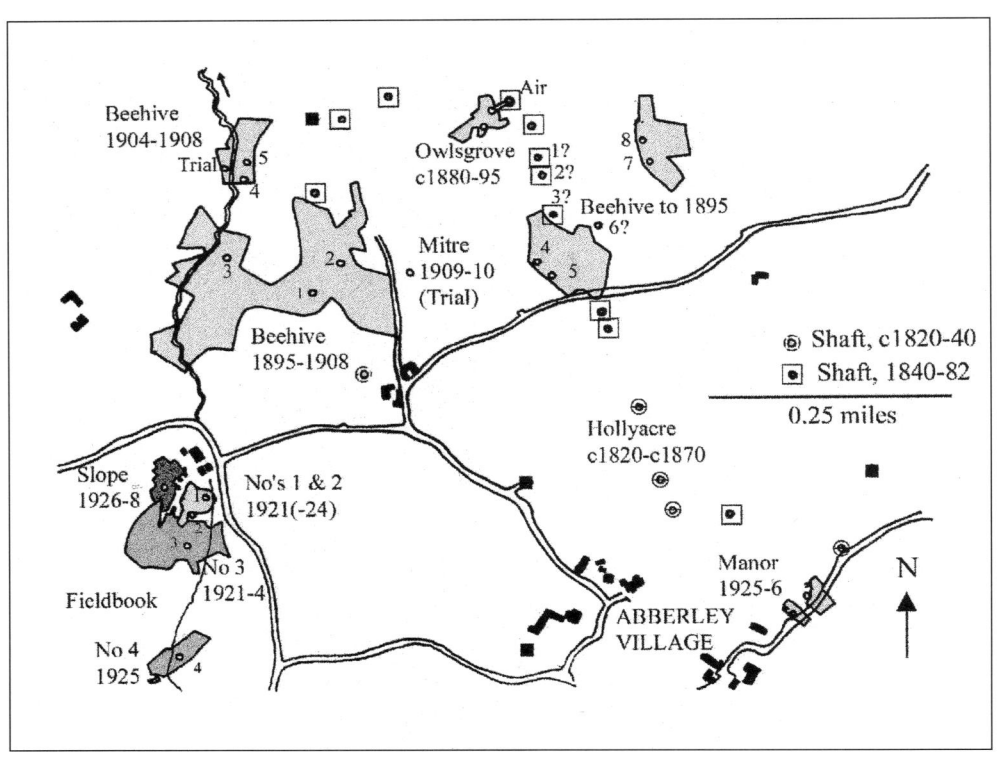

Mines of Abberley, c.1820-1920; east of the parish. Shaded areas are underground workings.

Beehive Colliery, Abberley, c.1900. The building on the left houses a beam engine that drives the winder for both shafts. The winding rope for the right-hand headgear is supported on vertical trestles. (Mr G. Norwood).

Hollyacre, leasing the mineral rights from the various owners. If the records are to be taken at face value, he did cease mining from 1872-1880 before starting again at Beehive farm. The coal here was worked from various shafts, not always connected, and by the turn of the century operations were being conducted from two physically separate mines, each with their own undermanager. Workings were in both the Main Sulphur and Hard Mine. In 1898 Henry Johnson noted 'great rejoicing' when a shaft was sunk into apparently sweet coal. At this period there was great interest in trying to prove the existence of sweet coal beneath the sulphur measures. As ever, the sweet coal quickly proved itself to be part of the well-established Hard Mine seam. Norwood's activities ended by 1910[12].

Norwood's enterprise, while small-scale, was reasonably well equipped, probably with steam winding from at least the 1860s. By contrast, at Pool House, matters were much less sophisticated. The mines were part of the Abberley Hall estate and run in conjunction with limekilns, quarries, a brickyard, as well as farms and cottages, under the overall supervision of an agent. In turn, he left the day-to-day running of the mine to a manager. In 1864 the manager appeared to do as little as possible. A man was killed in that year, 60 yards from the pit bottom.

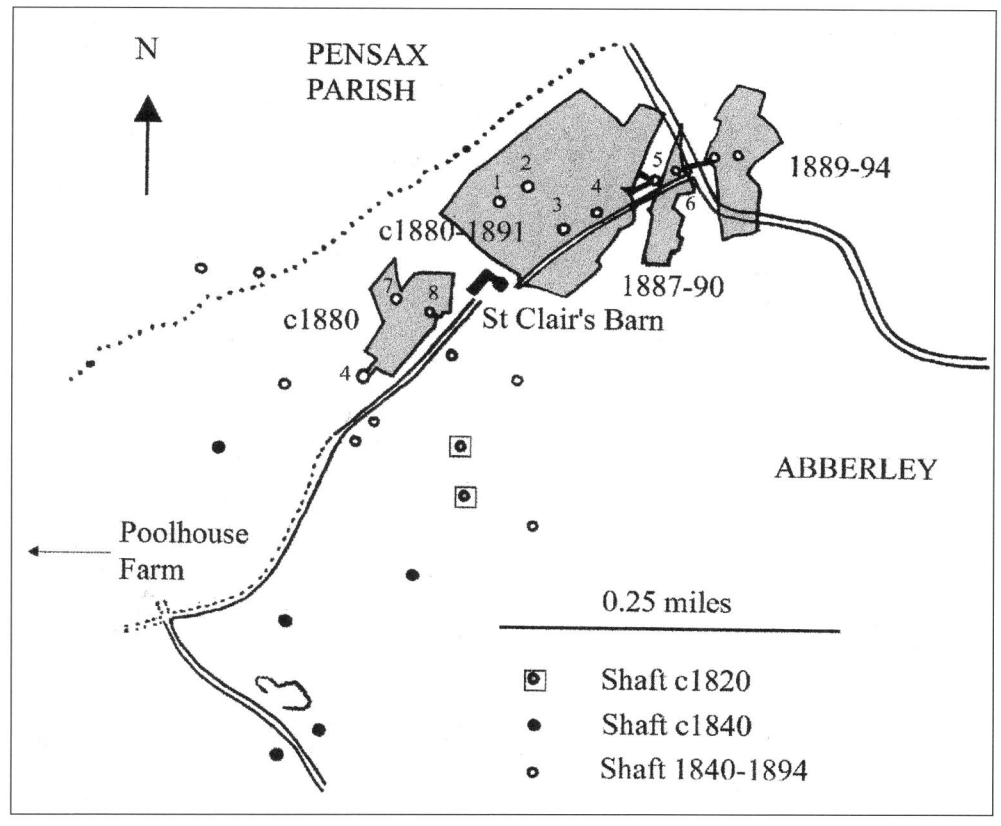

Poolhouse Colliery. Shaded areas are underground workings.

He was getting coal from a 4ft wide face, and had gone for 9ft without setting a prop to hold up the roof. Predictably, it fell and killed him. At the resulting inquest, the manager acknowledged that the pit had rules available, designed to prevent this type of accident, 'if the men wished to consult them', but they usually 'looked after themselves'. When the estate was sold to Joseph Jones of Oldham in 1868, an inventory showed four pits at work, all hand wound[13].

Jones, by 1875, had decided to end direct working of the mines, and in that year leased Bromley, Abberley and Cinderhill pits (probably all those at work at Poolhouse at the time) to John Bailey, for fifteen years at a royalty of 1s per ton coal and 6d per ton slack. The next year the lessees were John Booth and James Hardcastle his son-in-law; like Jones, they were both from Oldham. By 1883 Hardcastle had sole charge of the mine but little changed. Horse gins and hand windlasses continued to be used for at least some of the winding, with scant regard for safety. A fatal accident at No.9 pit in 1880 during water winding was attributed to neglect by Hardcastle and his banksman. A similar accident in 1883 when a man fell 48 yards down No.11 pit revealed the old culture still at work: the inquest was told it was each mans custom to tie his own knot in the winding rope to attach this to the skip in which he was to ride. In 1885, Hardcastle's defence to charges of working a mine with just one shaft and not having a proper winding apparatus was that it would not pay to spend £200 to sink a second shaft, and that he had lost £1,500 at the mine. This defence was not accepted by the magistrates[14].

Despite his pleas of poverty, Hardcastle not only worked Poolhouse until his lease expired in 1890, but then negotiated a new fourteen-year lease with powers to sink a new mine with steam winding. William Jones, the then estate owner, was to meet half the costs. This did not go well. First flooding caused the work to be postponed and then Hardcastle appeared to lose interest in the project. In despair Jones turned to Hardcastle's manager, Samson Yarnold. After much further wrangling between Hardcastle and Jones, the former finally agreed to go in 1893 and the leases were now made out in Yarnold's favour. The new works at Poolhouse were little more than a holding exercise as the ground had seen intensive mining for well over half a century. Accordingly, Yarnold was given a new lease in virgin ground, a mile to the north at Hollins, in 1894. Here, after overcoming problems due to water, coal was struck on 18 November 1895. Rapid progress was subsequently made, and by the turn of the century Hollins stood as a small but well-equipped and well-managed colliery, with the prospect of a profitable future in front of it[15]. It did indeed lead a prosperous and largely uneventful life for the next thirty years. In 1930 Yarnold retired and the mine and its mineral leases were acquired by the Bayton Colliery Company (see below). They eventually closed it in 1935; plans for further sinkings in the Abberley/Pensax area were scuppered by the Second World War. This final phase in the mining history of Pensax and Abberley is dealt with in more detail in the next chapter, in the account of the history of the Bayton Mining Company.

Back in Abberley itself there were attempts to revive the mining industry in the 1920s, largely as a result of the efforts of the owner of the Abberley Estate, Captain Astley Jones. The first of these mines was opened at Fieldbrook in 1922, adjacent to a brickworks. It was claimed that the mine employed fifty men, but it had an erratic career, being worked from a number of shafts and adits intermittently until 1929, latterly by the brickworks owners, Hurdis and Fletcher. The deepest shaft was No.4, 7ft diameter and reaching 78 yards to the Hard Mine. This closed due to flooding. Although Fieldbrook was not a great success, Jones was not put off, and in 1925 sank two pits at Manor and Newlands. Manor was abandoned in 1925, and Newlands produced nothing but water. Coal was only reached by a boring from the bottom of a 73-yard deep shaft; the second shaft never got below 30 yards. Jones's final fling was at Porchbrook ('Monkey's Island'), apparently sunk on the advice of A.R. Buffrey, long-time manager at Bayton, but who for a time worked for Jones. A small area of the Old Hall bats was worked, 3ft thick, but conditions were said to have been grim, and closure came quickly. However, Jones was remembered for many years with gratitude for his attempts to revive the mining industry and to provide employment[16].

In Rock, the first records that survive are from the middle of the eighteenth century. These show that collieries were open in the east of the parish by Rockmoor

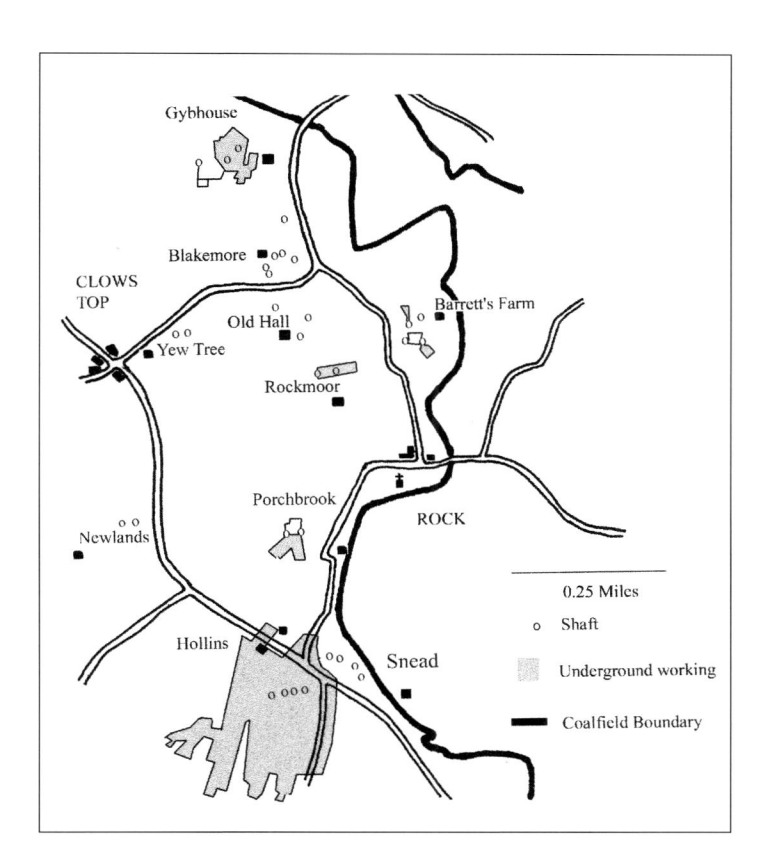

Mines of Rock and district, c.1850-1930. Shaded areas are underground workings.

and in the west at Snead Common and Stildon[17]. However, it is probable that mining was rather limited. The stratum at the eastern rim of the coalfield dips much more steeply from the outcrop compared to the western outcrop. Consequently there would be little scope for the development of the small shallow pits that characterized Mamble; mining here would need more capital investment to pay. However, by the mid-nineteenth century there were three mines in operation on the eastern side of the coalfield; Blakemoor, Gybhouse and Oldhall, and these were to continue in operation on-and-off until the end of the century[18]. Blakemoor was largely developed by Richard Davies, the owner and farmer, around 1841 and his widow Mary continued his work after his death. Blakemoor was at this time one of the mines most regularly in production, with Mary engaging a variety of lessees. In 1859-61 it and an associated brickyard were in the occupation of Messrs Marsh and Waterfield. In 1866 it was reported to be in the hands of William Dixon & Co., although in April of that year one John Morgan was prosecuted for failing to observe safety regulations regarding a steam engine at the mine. In 1867, a Liverpool-based company apparently leased the mine with the intention of sinking for deeper seams. The constant change of lessees does suggest that the mine had its problems. Nonetheless, in the early 1870s William Davis acquired both mine and farm, probably on the death of Mary. Davis did not keep Blakemoor open for long, but appears to have been casting covetous eyes on the Old Hall estate immediately to the south. This he purchased in 1877[19].

Old Hall was another farm-and-colliery enterprise, owned for many years by Edward Ree. The mine was associated with a brick-works and Ree also found time to run an inn, 'The Colliers Arms', and the local post-office. Some local entrepreneurs did not lack energy. Ree let the working of the mine out to Joseph Hopcutt and family, a local dynasty of miners. Although coal had been worked at Old Hall prior to 1841, in 1855 there was new development with the discovery of an additional seam of coal (celebrated in traditional style with a banquet hosted by Hopcutt and Ree). Two years later Hopcutt had less cause for celebration when his son was killed by the steam-winding engine. This was being worked by a fourteen year old boy who had been left on his own after eleven days supervision by his father. Safety, however, was not a priority for Hopcutt, for in 1866 he received a number of summonses, including one for failing to fence the winding engine properly. In 1868 a local guidebook claimed that Old Hall and Blakemoor were the two most important mines in the vicinity, but one had been forced to close due to it being flooded out by water from the other. This setback must only have been temporary, for both continued into the 1870s[20].

Following Ree's death in 1875, his estate was administered for a period by his brother Joseph. Surviving accounts suggest that the brickworks was profitable but the mine was now making a loss. In spite of this, it was purchased by William Davis of Blakemoor, although it was closed by flooding in 1881. In 1883 it was purchased by William Bickley who either deepened or sank a new shaft to give the mine extra life. In the 1890s it was purchased by Messrs Lindsay and Slater. Despite Bickley's earlier effort, the colliery must have now been in a very run-down state, and was judged so dangerous that HM Inspector of Mines refused to go underground on his first visit. A subsequent inspection revealed the return airway shrunk to the size of a 'rabbit hole', the roads full of broken timber and the air so stale that a candle could barely stay alight. Alexander Slater tried to blame the state of affairs on his manager, Cornelius Broom, and the next year gave up the lease to Broom. With this, the number of men employed at the pit fell from twenty to four, and it was abandoned in 1900[21].

Gybhouse farm and associated colliery were offered for sale in 1851. It was claimed that two acres of a 5ft seam had already been worked, at a profit of £2,000. Stone was also said to exist on the estate. By the 1860s, the mine and farm were owned by William Hanbury. For a while the mine encouraged great expectations, when the coal reached a thickness of 15ft. Unfortunately this was due to the seam folding back on itself and the normal thickness was soon resumed. For most of the 1870s the mine is not recorded, but in 1881 Walter Baxter took up the lease and sank a new shaft. This was nearly halted by an influx of water at 20 yards depth, but after Baxter had inspected Old Hall, he decided to go on. With the help of a 400 gallon/minute capacity pump, coal was struck at 97 yards in July 1881 and this was greeted by the normal celebrations. Development was still going on in January 1882 when a sinker was killed by a wooden wedge, normally used to secure the pump, falling down the shaft, and in August of that year there was a second celebration on finding the coal. There was now talk of connecting the mine with a branch line to the Tenbury and Bewdley Railway, but this was probably the high point of the proceedings. The branch railway was not built and in 1884 William Davis, fresh from Old Hall, replaced Baxter as lessee. Davis, like many of his contemporaries, seems unconcerned by the details of mine management; George Mole, his engine driver, sued him for non-payment of wages and, after he gave the mine up in 1888, the Inspector of Mines commented on its poor state. Elijah Davies, the new lessee, was clearly also out of the same mould, for he was prosecuted the next year for failing to carry out any improvements. The mine closed in 1894[22].

A fourth mine in this region was at Rockmoor. A sale notice of 1841 is said to show a tramway leading from this mine to the road at Clows Top. However, there was little subsequent activity until much later. The owner, Frederick Rogers is recorded as operating a colliery in the late 1870s. This was not apparently very long-lived. In July 1890 one Thomas Byng announced in the local papers that he had re-opened the mine and could sell coal and coke. There were then a number of changes in lessee, until Joseph and Edwin Whitehouse, mining engineers and brickmakers of Bewdley and Coseley took over in 1892. By 1894 they had formed the Rockmoor Colliery Company, with £30,000 capital made up of 1,000 shares and mainly financed by a group of Knutsford businessmen. The Whitehouses were paid £11,200, largely in shares, for the colliery that consisted of a steam winding engine and two 35-yard shafts to a 5ft 6in coal seam. The new company at once took out an option to lease a lower seam. Sadly the concern ceased to trade in January 1896 with many of its shares unsubscribed[23].

Despite the failure of the Rockmoor Colliery Company, financial speculation involving it and its neighbours was only just beginning, thanks largely to the efforts of Thomas Dalley, a local businessman. By 1897 he had acquired the mineral leases to most of the north of the coalfield not in the Mawley or Shakenhurst estates. These included Rockmoor, Gybhouse and Blakemoor. He then floated the grandly named South Shropshire Coal, Coke, Brick and Railway Company Ltd. This proposed to upgrade the plant at Rockmoor to produce 5,000 tons of coal per annum, reopen Blakemoor to get 2,000 tons of coal each year with new shafts, build a brickworks, sixty new houses and a railway from the assorted works to Cleobury Station. Also included in the deal was a brickworks at Tipton; in all probability the only profitable part of the whole enterprise. The share-buying public remained sceptical and the venture crashed. Next year Dalley was back. He put down a 295ft borehole at Blakemoor while suspending the vestigial mining taking place at Rockmoor. In July 1898 he began a deep sinking at Yew Tree, near Clows Top, and when a 3ft 6in seam was struck the next month, coal samples were sent to Kidderminster for analysis. In spite of the best efforts of a sinker who went too close to a gunpowder charge with a lighted candle, Yew Tree penetrated further seams at depth, eventually reaching one considered to be of sulphur-free coal by Henry Johnson, an eminent mining engineer. At this time Johnson had also proclaimed coal in Abberley to be sulphur-free; he was wrong about both seams. However, on the strength of these results Dalley floated the Wyre Forest Coal and Clay Fields Development Ltd; a similar scheme to its predecessor but without the Tipton works and with £50,000 capital, making it only half as expensive. It also included the Yew Tree sinking. Of this capital, £28,000 was to be paid to Dalley himself for expenses in developing the estates. Sadly for Dalley, this company faired no better than its predecessor, and all works were abandoned by 1899. Nonetheless, as late as 1902 there was still talk of an area of sweet coal around Rock, largely, it appears, the idea of Arthur Auden, a Bewdley-based mining engineer, and there may have been hope of reviving the grandiose plans of Dalley. If so, they never came to fruition[24].

The first decade of the twentieth century saw very little mining activity in Rock, apart from nebulous trials at Snead. However, as elsewhere, the 1920s saw a final if short-lived revival of the industry. In 1922, J.H. Armishaw made a trial at Birch Hill Farm. At Old Hall the next year John Clarke & Sons of Dudley made an abortive attempt at mining and from 1923-1925 an 'Old Hall Mining Company' was active at Barretts Farm. They worked the euphemistically named Silver Brooch seam, allegedly sulphur free. In fact this was probably no more than the Main Sulphur worked elsewhere[25]. In 1929 the Mole family took a ten-year lease on the minerals under the Old Hall Estate. The Moles were at this time haulage contractors at Clows Top, but they were of good local mining stock with ambitions to become mine owners. At Old Hall they found little coal, but they did get what was claimed to be fireclay. Analysis unfortunately showed that it had no refractory properties and was good only for normal pottery. After this, relations between the Moles and the landlord, A.R. Morris deteriorated and mining ceased in 1931[26]. The Moles were ultimately to have their day elsewhere. A pair of shafts were sunk at Stildon in the early 1930s by the Bayton Colliery Company, but these are dealt with in the next chapter; suffice it to say they were sunk for exploratory purposes and no coal was ever mined from them.

There are two footnotes to this review of the industry in Rock. Firstly, it is instructive to examine developments in the adjacent community of Far Forest, part of Rock parish in the nineteenth century. Nowhere is the spirit of speculation that characterized the Wyre Forest in Victorian times better illustrated than by examining a series of trials made here, in the Dowles valley. This is barren ground with no workable coal. However, hope reigned eternal and local commentators did their best to encourage this. A guidebook of the 1860s spoke of 'large quantities' of coal that had been found during the construction of the Tenbury and Bewdley railway and also said that the district had a canal that could be used to take away the coal. The truth was that a rather thin seam had been cut through during work on the western edge of the coalfield at Prizeley, where old workings caused some subsidence. The Leominster Canal had been drained and partly obliterated by the railway! By the late 1860s it was reported that the Crown Estates had sold off large areas of the woods and these had been snapped up by South Staffordshire entrepreneurs, eager for coal[27]. The Crown Estates were in truth much more concerned to be protected from any liability that might arise from mining. In 1874, Sir George Elliot was said to be boring for coal on his lands at Alton. Elliot privately denied the story. Nonetheless, some real exploration was carried out. In about 1875, James Higginbottom of Pensax put down a borehole on some of his land at Coventry Mill in search of coal. In 1876, four Staffordshire businessmen formed a consortium to try and find the thick coal at Town Mill. In 1896 Captain Childe of Kinlet attempted to find the continuation of the Brooch coal under Park Wood, then being got much further north on his lands on the Highley-Kinlet boundary. As late as 1910 another borehole was put down close to the Dowles at Alton. None of these ever found an ounce of workable coal[28].

A second footnote comes from this century and concerns the experiments with coal gasification. The idea behind this was to convert the coal to gas underground (by partial combustion) which would then be pumped to the surface for use above ground. Trials had been conducted in a variety of countries and early experiments by the Ministry of Fuel and Power were conducted at Chesterfield. In 1951, a site at Rockmoor was selected for further development work. The underlying technique was to drill two or more parallel lines of boreholes into the seam and then attempt to ignite the coal lying in between the holes. High-pressure linkage involved a bag of coal being set alight by electricity and then forcing the fire forwards by high pressure air. This failed because the large number of minor faults present dissipated the air. Electric linkage was then tried; current at 1.5MV was passed between two electrodes to produce an underground electric fire. The best results gassified 200 tons of coal in $2\frac{1}{2}$ months. The apparatus for this was then moved to Chesterfield and a third technique was tried. Two shafts were sunk and two parallel horizontal galleries were laid out in the coal. They were then

Underground Gasification of Coal Experimental Installation at Rockmoor, operated by the Ministry of Power and Fuel in the 1950s. The photograph shows coal gas being burnt off. (J. Blood-Smith).

connected by a series of horizontal boreholes laid out by specialized contractors, Messrs. Boyles Drilling Co. A first trial in the Brock Hall seam was followed by the sinking of two 6ft 6in shafts 80ft into the Main Sulphur. The two galleries were 200ft apart and linked by four boreholes. Using air heated to 800°C, the coal was ignited and over thirteen weeks, 1,300 tons was gasified.[29]

The Minister of Fuel and Power visited the site in 1952, shortly after it had opened and it was expanded in 1953. In 1956 it was handed over to the NCB, who decided to concentrate work at the Newman Spinney site near Chesterfield. Rockmoor was run down and the site eventually cleared; some of the equipment found its way to the Mole brothers' mine at Hunthouse. One unusual memorial to the experiment is a miner's lamp, given to Rock church by the NCB in recognition of the role of the parish.[30]

7

BAYTON AND MAMBLE

In Mamble, as early as 1644 the name 'coalpit field' occurs at Westwood farm on the Shakenhurst estate of the Mersey family. However, the largest mines were to be on the adjacent Mawley estate of the Blount family. Mining seems to have started here sometime between 1700 and 1720 and it was to continue almost without interruption until 1925[1]. In 1771 the mines under the Blount estates at Mamble and Woodside in Bayton were leased to a Francis Bint who spent in excess of £1,000 in laying out adits. Unfortunately for him, he had to surrender his lease in 1778. Coal was being worked on the adjoining Mersey family estates also in Bayton and Mamble at about this time, although details are obscure. An adit had been driven by the early nineteenth century to drain the mines under the small Newlands estate in Mamble[2]. Blount's mines received a boost with the opening of the Leominster Canal from Southnett Wharf near Mamble, first to Tenbury and then to Leominster. The first boats on the canal carried coal from Mamble, and there was steady traffic throughout the first half of the nineteenth century[3]. Blount was a major shareholder in the Leominster Canal, with 1,000 shares and for him the failure to complete the canal to Stourport was probably a great bonus; it gave him exclusive access to the Teme Valley and Leominster markets, shutting out all his competitors. Indeed, some shareholders complained that a number of the directors stood to benefit from this arrangement that ensured Leominster with constant coal and Blount with constant revenue[4]. The mines themselves moved relentlessly eastwards from the outcrop, following the coal. New shafts were sunk every few acres and these relied entirely on winding by hand. Some change must have come about by the start of the 1860s, when the Leominster canal was finally drained, depriving the mines of their outlet to the Teme Valley. It seems likely that the plateway system leading to the canal was initially retained for internal transport to a landsale wharf on the Tenbury turnpike. However, this had been dismantled by 1881 and from this date the coal must simply have been purchased at the pithead and loaded straight into carts[5].

From probably at least the 1820s, a second site on the Blount estates was worked for coal at Buckets Leasow[6]. These mines showed the same lack of

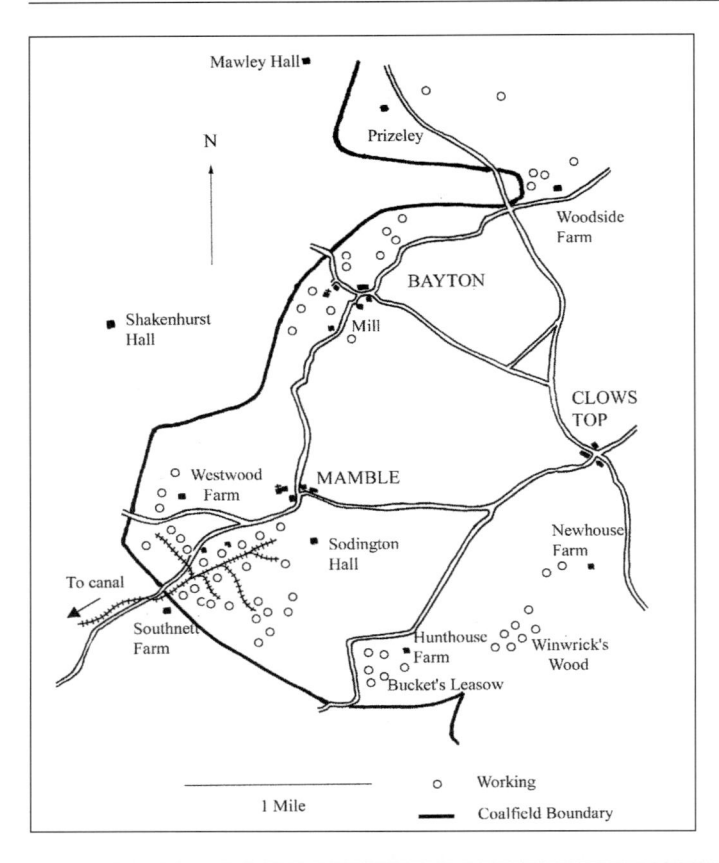

Mines of Bayton and Mamble, c.1800.

Underground at Buckets Leasow, c.1900. The young man on the left is Edward Aston Jnr, the son of the colliery owner. The photograph was lit by magnesium tape flash. Note the candle stuck to the roof support in the centre of the picture.

technical refinement as their cousins just over the hill at Mamble itself; indeed, they were probably only ever landsale mines with no plateway system. At some point (probably before 1870), Blount bored for coal at Carton Hall on his land, but no mining resulted from this[7]. A major administrative change seems to have come about in 1869, when Blount abandoned direct control of all his collieries and leased them to Thomas Aston. It is likely that the Aston family were the principal contractors when Blount controlled the mines directly. With increasing competition from both larger neighbouring collieries and also rail-borne coal from outside the district, it seems surprising that Thomas, and later his son Edward, managed to survive. However, both Buckets Leasow and Mamble continued into the twentieth century. The Aston's also worked Upper Moorend Farm, and this, with the collieries, gave them a good living. In spite of their apparent crudeness, the pits at Mamble and Buckets Leasow out-performed many of their better-equipped competitors[8]. Buckets Leasow finally closed in 1908; Mamble survived the Great War until 1925. Shortly before its closure a local newspaper described it as 'one of the most profitable small mines in the country'[9]. Indeed its closure was not due to economics but to the rise of the Bayton Colliery Company, as will be seen shortly.

In Bayton it is very difficult to discover much about the coal industry before the middle of the nineteenth century. A collier is first recorded in the parish register in 1609 and there are frequent mentions in the eighteenth century. In the late eighteenth and early nineteenth centuries there are mentions of estates where the presence of coal was either known or suspected, but the real scale of working is hard to gauge. The first map drawn by the Ordnance Survey in 1817 shows a scatter of shafts throughout the village. By the 1830s a colliery was at work on 'Almshouse Meadow', but it has not proved possible to identify this location[10]. From the 1860s onwards it is possible to identify two distinct groups of pits. In the north of the parish were the mines of the Shakenhurst estate, while in the south was the Glebe Colliery, close to the Bayton-Mamble road. Little can be said about the Shakenhurst mines beyond listing their lessees, but it is possible to trace the Glebe Colliery in a little more detail. It was owned by the long serving priest in charge of Bayton, the Revd David Davies. He employed a variety of contractors to work the mine; Ashton and Wyatt in 1859, for example. By this date, or shortly afterwards, a steam engine was at work over one shaft, but a hand-windlass remained at another one. There were two additional shafts that seem to have only been used for ventilation. In 1863, Davies paid John Wyatt for driving a level between the engine pit and another shaft and a year later he paid compensation for subsidence caused to the Bayton-Mamble road as a result of his workings. When Davies died in 1875, the brick engine house was reported to be in need of repair[11].

After Davies's death, no more is heard of Glebe Colliery, but the Mill Colliery, owned by John Cook, now features in the records. Cook had probably worked a little coal before this time, but in 1873 he leased his coal to Cornelius and Thomas Broom and James Hadwell. It seems likely that this was adjacent to Glebe. After many problems the mine was taken over by William Wyatt in 1876. A plan of 1880 shows five shafts adjacent to the Bayton-Mamble road, with a steam winder at one of these and workings in three seams. Mill Colliery continued in use until 1899, although at the end it employed only three men underground and two on the surface. Wyatt also kept a shop in Bayton but at this time he was reported as 'bankrupt and not worth a farthing'. It is unlikely Mill Colliery helped his finances and its demise was not unexpected[12].

The detailed history of the Shakenhurst estate mines can be traced from 1895 onwards. At this date William Lawton Viggars obtained the mineral leases to most of the estate and sank shafts just south of the church. Viggars was a partner in the Highley Mining Company who had revolutionized the industry in the north of the coalfield with a deep, modern sinking. Quite what attracted him to Bayton is not clear; in Highley he apparently led a prosperous life as gentleman farmer and pillar of the community. The Church Pits were worked out in 1900 and Viggars sank new shafts in the village centre. The next year he formed the Bayton Coal, Coke and Brick Company to purchase his interest in the mine. This was almost entirely composed of shareholders in the Highley Mining Company, who perhaps should have known better than to be dabbling in the Bayton area. They quickly lived to regret their involvement, for the company was moribund within a year[13]. Viggars himself was slightly burnt in an underground explosion in 1902 and gave up the mine in 1903.

In 1904 the Shakenhurst mining lease was taken over by one James Smallshaw, of Arscott Colliery near Shrewsbury. The coal worked by Smallshaw at Arscott was of a similar type to that at Bayton, and perhaps this experience helped him succeed where Viggars had failed. Smallshaw took over two new shafts in the north-east of the village. By 1907 his Bayton Colliery was profitable enough for him to resurrect the idea of a railway link to the Great Western Railway at Cleobury Mortimer. In the event nothing came of this and Smallshaw left in 1910[14]. Francis Whitworth Wright then purchased the colliery in August 1911. Wright was a mining engineer who moved from Halifax to start a small, short-lived mine near his new house at Snead in 1910. He was also a director of the Cowie Harbour Company in North Borneo. At Bayton he expanded the workforce to about seventy and finally obtained a connection with the Great Western Railway via an aerial ropeway constructed by R. White & Son in 1912. At the colliery he began to mechanize by introducing compressed air, probably for the first time in the coalfield[15].

As befitted a director of a company located in the distant reaches of the Empire, Wright's horizons were not just limited to Bayton Colliery and the Shakenhurst estate. Adjacent to that estate lay the lands of Mawley Hall belonging to Sir Walter Blount; 1,500 acres in the centre of the coalfield, much of it untouched and with only a small fraction being mined by Edward Aston at Mamble. This represented the future for Wright. To help him get it, he must have felt that he needed more backing. Accordingly he began to search for partners in 1913 and was introduced to Vincent and Ernest Bramall. Vincent was a Lancashire mining engineer and a

Bayton Aerial Ropeway, erected in 1912 by R. White and Sons of Widnes. It operated until the closure of Bayton No.1 pit. The ropeway was 2,443 yards long and ran from the colliery to the sidings at Cleobury Mortimer station. In order to avoid crossing the Cleobury to Clows Top road where it lay in Shropshire, an angle station was constructed which allowed the ropeway to cross the road in Worcestershire. The photograph shows the discharge terminus at Cleobury Mortimer station.

The angle station where the ropeway changed direction. There was a lot of spillage of coal at this point and the recovered coal was sold from here.

The loading terminal at Bayton Colliery, with a loaded bucket starting on its journey. The ropeway was powered by a steam engine fed by the colliery boilers.

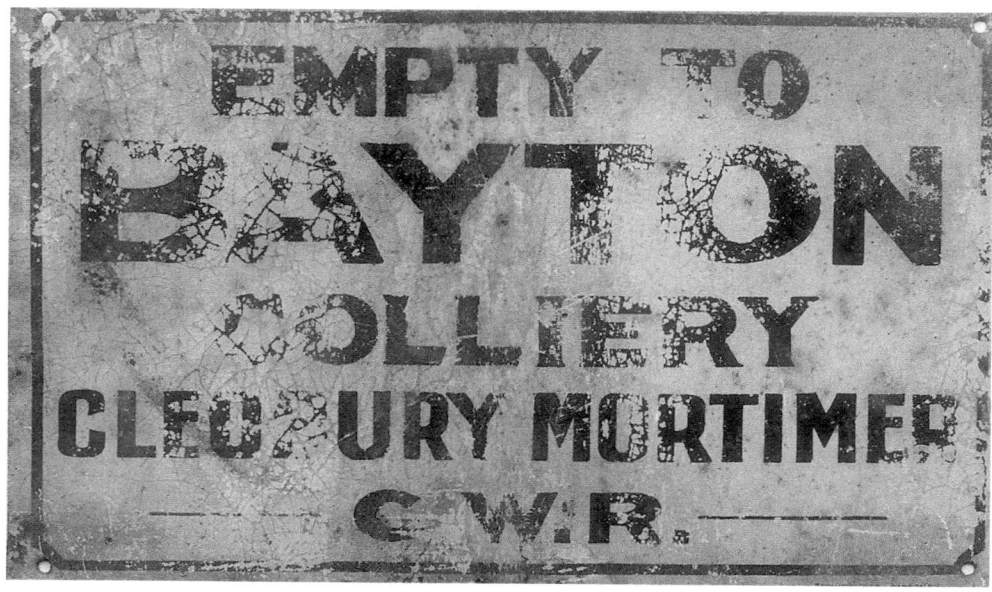

Wagon empty return instruction plate, Bayton Colliery, 1920.

co-partner with his brother Ernest in the large Desford Colliery in Leicestershire. They together formed the Bayton Colliery Company, registered in December 1914 with £8,000 capital. The company's aims were to conclude negotiations with Sir Walter Blount as speedily as possible and sink a new mine on his land, allowing Bayton to be abandoned. The First World War put a stop to any progress; Wright, Blount and a third of the company's workforce all departed for the front. At Bayton, the Main Sulphur Coal had been exhausted and the company were forced to get the Hard Mine; a tough coal that was difficult to work, but which was a popular household fuel and which stood up well to the rigours of transport by aerial ropeway and railway wagon. Mechanization continued, with the compressed air used to drive parts of the underground haulage and heading machine. In 1916 extra mineral leases were taken out over a small area in Bayton. In spite of this, the company complained that the mine was unprofitable. However, increasingly matters were taken out of its hands as the Government regulated the industry, a state of affairs that did not cease until 1920.[16]

Deregulation of the industry almost coincided with the final agreement with Sir Walter Blount over the Mawley leases. These were signed in 1921 and, with the removal of Government support and near exhaustion of the Hard Mine at Bayton, the company wasted no time in starting a new sinking, Bayton No.2, just to the north of Mamble village. Rather curiously a single square, timber-lined shaft was sunk. The site was apparently chosen because of the ease of extending the aerial ropeway to it, but it soon became apparent that communication with outside markets would be irrelevant. The mine lay on the edge of the Mawley estate and unexpectedly the coal was found to be to the dip of the shaft. This meant that the workings rapidly filled with water. The drier coal to the rise of the shaft lay outside the leased area or was cut off by old workings. Although the coal was excellent, the poor underground conditions made closure inevitable in 1923, with the loss of £2,000 worth of investment. At the same time the old Bayton Colliery, Bayton No.1 finally exhausted the last of its reserves and also closed. The Bayton Colliery Company was left without that most basic of assets, a working colliery[17].

Salvation for the company came with the opening of a drift mine into the Main Sulphur Coal as it outcropped in Winwrick's Wood, by the banks of the Dumbleton Brook. Although there had been outcrop working here, it had not amounted to much and there appeared to be easy pickings left. Given the perilous state of the company's finances, this was what was needed. In the event the mine exceeded expectations; it became evident that there were extensive reserves of good quality household fuel. The following year a tramway was laid from the mines to the main road and this proved to be a timely investment. In 1926 the pit worked all the way through the general strike and for a period must have been practically the only source of coal within a fifty-mile radius. Demand was so great that a second drift was opened to the south of the first one and in 1927 the company started its own haulage business, selling direct to the customers using a fleet of twelve one-ton Ford trucks and a seven-ton Clayton and Shuttleworth steam lorry. The aerial ropeway from Bayton No.1 was eventually dismantled,

This and the photograph below form a panorama of the drift mines in Winwrick's Wood in 1928. Above are the square timbered entry to the empties tunnel on the left and the steel arched loaded tunnel on the extreme right. (G. Bramall).

The second half of the Winwrick's Wood panorama shows the Robey boiler which provided steam for the haulage engines. In the background is the tub haulage incline. (G. Bramall).

The tub haulage incline from the drifts in Winwrick's Wood to the screens and Gypsy Lane. The steam engine on the left hauled full tubs of coal up from the workings and empty tubs brought the haulage rope back down. (G. Bramall).

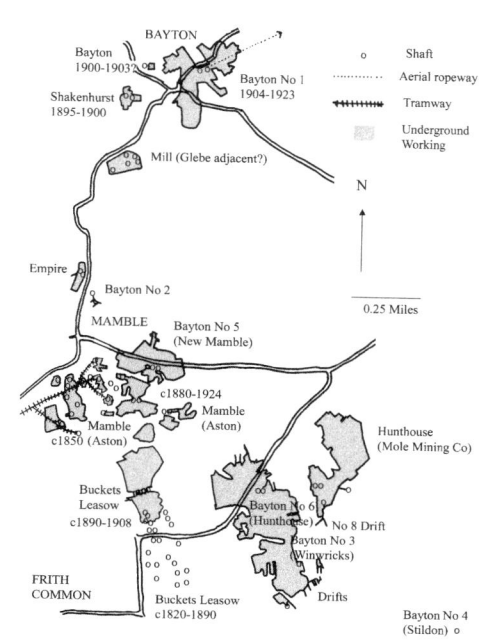

Mines of Bayton and Mamble, c.1850-1972. Shaded areas are underground workings.

Screens at Gypsy Lane (later to be the site of No.6 pit), sorting the coal from the drifts in Winwrick's Wood, 1926. (G. Bramall).

although the exchange sidings at Cleobury Station were turned into a brickworks owned by the company. As the drift workings became more extensive, it was decided to sink two shafts into these to facilitate operations. In the event only one shaft was put down, being completed in 1929, but this was then used for coal winding. A road was put down to the pit head so lorries could be loaded directly and the tramway was abandoned[18].

A by-product of the success of the Bayton Colliery was the demise of Edward Aston's operations at Mamble. Aston nominally worked his mine here by virtue of a lease of 1869. However, the colliery had long since exceeded the boundaries specified in this document. While Aston was the only mining tenant of the Mawley Estate this was of no real consequence, but after the minerals under the rest of the estate were let to the Bayton Colliery Company it was another matter. The issue did not come to a head until late 1924 and Aston then closed the pit and filled it in before a proper inspection could be done. Although this marked the end of the old Mamble Colliery, it was not quite the end of Aston's career in mining. Shortly before the storm at Mamble erupted, he had secured a lease on the neighbouring Shakenhurst Estate, ironically taking over leases which had just been vacated by the Bayton Colliery Company. Aston sank the Empire Colliery half way between Bayton and Mamble in 1924, with technical assistance from Samson Yarnold of Hollins Colliery. Unfortunately it was not a success and closed the following year[19]. There was to be one last fling on the Shakenhurst estate, involving the Mole family. Throughout the 1920s they had been involved in a number of ventures in Rock. In 1933 they turned their attention to the Shakenhurst estate with a trial borehole that showed promise. As the costs of a full sinking were too great for the Moles alone, in 1935 they entered into partnership

Empire Colliery, owned by Edward Aston. The two headgears were wound from a single steam engine. The winding rope for the foreground shaft – upcast and water delivery – is supported by a jockey pulley on a pole. Water was drawn from the workings by lowering the steel tank or bowke into the sump at the shaft bottom. When the full tank reached the surface a shuttle was opened and the load of water poured out and ran down the steel chute, clear of the shaft.

with E.J. & J. Pearson Ltd, a large manufacturer of firebrick from Stourbridge. (It was Pearsons who had tested the clay from Old Hall for the Moles a few years earlier; see previous chapter). In 1937 Pearsons assumed full responsibility for operations, and contracted with Andrew Kyle Ltd of Ayrshire to further test the strata by means of a borehole. No fireclay was located, but two seams of coal were found close to the bottom of their shaft. However, as Pearsons had three other pits in Stourbridge, one of which was doing particularly well, they decided they no longer needed extra supplies and so did no more at Shakenhurst[20].

Returning to the story of the Bayton Colliery Company, with their position secured by the success at Winwrick's Wood (or Bayton No.3 as it was officially called), work was now done to explore other areas within the Mawley Estate. This assumed new importance in the light of fears that the 1930 Coal Mines Act would restrict the opening of new shafts. To make sure that this did not happen, a new sinking was undertaken at Stildon Manor (Bayton No.4), largely to stake a claim in a previously undeveloped area. This demonstrated that the upper seam (or Old Hall Bats as it was known locally) was workable in this locality. However, the need to develop Stildon vanished when Samson Yarnold offered Hollins Colliery for sale. Hollins was not regarded as a particularly attractive proposition as a mine, but following the 1930 Coal Mines Act, a highly regulated selling and marketing scheme had been set up, with each colliery company allocated a sales quota. By purchasing Hollins, the Bayton Colliery Company also obtained its quota, at a time when they were keen to expand production. With Hollins also came the opportunity to acquire the mineral rights of the Abberley estate, and when this was done the Bayton Colliery Company had an almost unassailable position in the south of the coalfield. In the short term, it was decided to keep Hollins open as long it continued to make money. In the longer term there were plans for a replacement sinking on the Abberley Estate, and ultimately, further development at Stildon[21].

The next move came in 1934-1935, with the sinking of New Mamble, or Bayton No.5. The end for Hollins finally came in December of that year, due to difficulties with the downcast shaft, and the men were transferred to New Mamble. Unfortunately, it did not take long to realise that there were also problems at New Mamble. The coal was good, but the roof and floor were soft, making it difficult to maintain roads. Additionally, and unexpectedly, it was found that the pit was on the dip-side of Aston's flooded workings from his old Mamble Colliery. Consequently, the water from these would naturally drain into the new pit; an ironic final victory perhaps for Aston, following his eviction from the mines by the Bayton Colliery Company ten years previously. A compressed air driven coal cutter failed to cut costs and it became obvious that New Mamble was destined for an unhappy life. Unfortunately for the company, that life was far from short[22].

The response of the Bayton Colliery Company to the problems at New Mamble was essentially three-fold. In the short term there was little option but to soldier on with the pit, trying to work it as economically as possible. However, at Winwrick's Wood Colliery, Bayton No.3, there was scope for further investment. The mine was profitable but rather simple, with no compressed air available to work machinery underground, and no ponies so that all tramming was done by hand. A decision was taken to sink further shafts to replace the one put down in 1929, and to couple this with a modernization programme to increase output. This formed the medium-term part of the company's strategy. In the long term there were plans for a new sinking on the Abberley estate to replace Hollins. This, together with the redevelopment of Bayton No.3, would allow the closure of New Mamble.

Shaft sinking for the new extension of Bayton No.3, to be called Hunthouse Colliery, or Bayton No.6, began in April 1936, and by mid-1937 one shaft was completed and the other was halfway down. The winding engine and boilers for the work had been salvaged from Hollins, a typical piece of thrift on the part of the company. For the first time compressed air picks were used underground and were a great success. Then came an unexpected problem. Water had been met with in the sinking of the shaft at Bayton No.3, but had been dealt with by means of coffering (i.e. sealing the area around the water with concrete), without causing any particular problems. However, in August 1937 it broke through a minor fault and flooded the workings. Pumping the mine dry again would have

Bayton No.3 shaft in 1929. This was sunk to intercept the drift mine workings in Winwrick's Wood. On the left is the incline from these drifts. The vertical boiler came from an earlier Bayton Colliery. (G. Bramall).

The River Severn in flood at Beales Corner, Bewdley, 1937. The Bayton Colliery Company coal wagon gets through with bags of coal for Kidderminster customers.

Bayton No.6 Colliery 1938. The right-hand headgear served the downcast and coal winding shaft. There was no fan installed; the workings were ventilated by a natural flow of air. (G. Bramall).

been very expensive and given the good progress being made with the new sinkings, it was decided to abandon the old mine, temporarily transferring all men to New Mamble until Bayton No.6 was ready. Despite working three shifts at New Mamble in order to get enough coal to keep the haulage business viable, it still lost money. Bayton No.6 finally was completed in June 1939, and immediately men were transferred to it from New Mamble, with a view to the rapid closure of the latter.

Once again, the plans of the Bayton Colliery Company were thwarted by circumstances. In September 1939 the Second World War started. Plans for an electric winder at No.6 were immediately frozen until after the war. Just as quickly, the Ministry of Fuel and Power took effective control of the mining industry, and refused to allow the company to close New Mamble, in spite of it being unprofitable. It was judged that coal was needed at any price. The reserves of the Main Sulphur became exhausted in 1941, and the workings moved into the lower, Hard Mine seam. The chief difficulty here was that only one shaft went down this far, and so it was necessary to sink a cross-measure drift. The problems that resulted from this arrangement ensured that the pit remained unprofitable. Even so, in 1943 the Ministry of Fuel and Power still refused to allow its closure. At Bayton No.6 good progress was made but in the absence of electricity the pit suffered from a lack of suitable power. This was eventually solved by the purchase of two gas engines that drove air compressors to power machinery underground. At this point, the pit was capable of accommodating all the men from New Mamble. However, agreement to close New Mamble only came in 1944 after the company agreed to open up drift mines for the men too old to work at the new

Mines of Winwrick's Wood, 1924-1972. Shaded areas are underground workings.

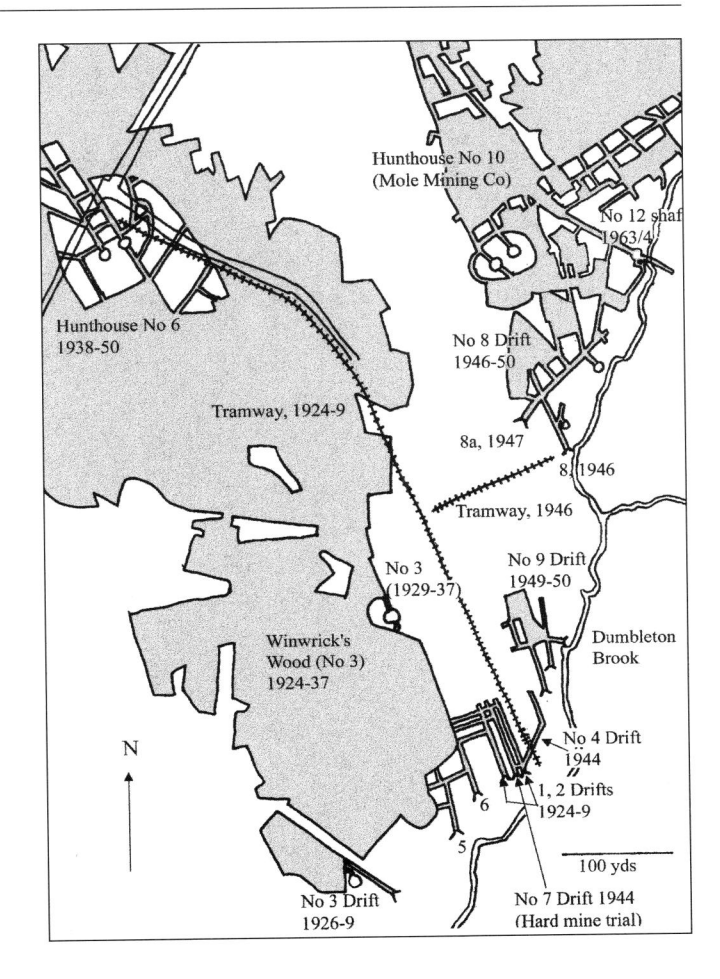

Bayton No.6, with the aim of cleaning out the old workings started in 1924. These had the bonus of allowing a more extensive exploration of the geology of Hunthouse Wood. It was discovered that the workings lay in a trough fault such that the Main Sulphur in the fault lay almost on the same horizon as the Hard Mine outside it. The practical implications were that it allowed Geoffrey Bramall, the managing director of the Bayton Colliery Company and its geologist, to locate a new area of Main Sulphur coal to the east of the existing workings[23].

The closure of New Mamble in 1944 lifted a significant burden from the Bayton Colliery Company. For the first time since 1936 it was freed of unprofitable mines and with the ending of the Second World War, the electricity supply arrived in November 1945. For the time being the steam winder was retained, as the frequency of power cuts was such that the electricity could not be relied upon for such an important job. The output of No.6 was typically 18,000 tons per annum, at a profit of about 4s per ton. In 1946 the results of the assorted trial drifts and sinkings to the east of the trough fault became apparent with the opening of a new drift mine, Bayton No.8. Initially this was reached via a rope-worked incline, but later a new entrance was made to the workings, to allow lorry access. Although the drift only employed a few men with an output of about 1,000 tons per annum, it was hoped that this could be expanded if the opportunity arose[24].

Against the good news coming from the mines there was the threat of nationalization from the post-war Labour government. Understandably, no colliery owner welcomed this, but unlike most, the Bayton Colliery Company thought it saw a way of avoiding it. By declaring itself a small mine, it could escape direct control and work under the terms of a special license issued by the National Coal Board. This worked for a short period. However, the NCB's definition of a small mine was not that of the Bayton Colliery Company. The NCB insisted that men had to be transferred from No.6 to the drifts, seriously compromising the viability of the larger mine. There were problems with the selling price the NCB deemed acceptable for Bayton coal, and also with the royalties payable back to the Board. This last point became particularly acute when flooding in February 1948 turned an average profit of 2s a ton into a loss of 5s a ton for the next six months. With no prospect of any long-term agreement with the NCB, the Bayton Colliery Company agreed to transfer the mine to the state-run concern, while retaining the brick yard and coal haulage businesses[25].

The Coal Board's tenure of Bayton No.6 and the associated drifts was to be a short and inglorious one. The long-serving manager, Walter Moody, was replaced; an act that caused considerable resentment and the loss of much good will. They further antagonized the work force by cutting the rates of the skilled day men. They instituted a number of changes in terms of machinery at the colliery, including the installation of an electric winder, new pumps and the replacement of compressed air picks with a coal cutter. None of these were a great success; for example, the coal cutters required extensive long-wall faces that could not be easily maintained. They also suffered from flooding. The mine was finally closed in February 1950, despite local opposition, with the men being transferred to either Beech Tree Colliery in Lye or Alveley. No serious attempt was made to work the drifts, although Bramall was twice refused permission to reopen them under license. The decision to close the colliery was backed by the Midland Area of the National Union of Mineworkers, which seems to have been motivated more by loyalty to the nationalized industry than to its members[26]. Ironically, within a few weeks of closing Hunthouse the NCB expressed an interest in open-cast mining in the area, but this was never followed up.

The most damning indictment of the NCB's management of Hunthouse was to come with the successful reworking of the area by a private mine. As noted elsewhere, the Mole family had long harboured ambitions to operate a mine. With the withdrawal of the NCB and the Bayton Colliery Company, they at last had the region to themselves. The most attractive proposition was to re-enter the coal that had been worked from the No.8 drift, previously identified by Geoffrey Bramall as being an area ripe for development. Accordingly, in 1954 the Mole Mining Company started work, and by 1956 had two shafts down and a face opened out.

Hunthouse Colliery, 1972, owned by the Mole Mining Company. The headgear on the right serves the downcast, coal winding shaft. The electric winders are housed in the pre-fabricated building between the headgears. The workings were ventilated with an ex-Royal Navy electric fan, sited at the upcast shaft.

Hunthouse Colliery, 1970; an empty tub pushed off the cage at the pit bottom by Charlie Weaver. (Sunday Mercury).

Hunthouse Colliery, 1970. Jack Jenkins and George Dudlick at the coal face (Sunday Mercury).

The mine first of all cleaned out the area to the limits of the drifts, and then moved into new territory to the north and east. The pit was worked as a small mine, under licence from the NCB, and thereby limited to thirty men. With an electric winder and compressed air picks at the face, output was 30-50 tons a day. In 1963 an additional shaft was sunk and fitted with a pump to improve drainage. The mine worked well for nearly twenty years. The end came when a newly opened longwall face struck water, leading to rapid flooding. It was judged not worth trying to recover the mine. The Mole Mining Company was briefly succeeded by a short-lived workers co-operative which failed in February 1972. The Arab-Israeli war later that year saw the quadrupling of oil prices, and was followed by several attempts to sell the mine as a going concern. Unfortunately, none of these had any practical results, although the site was not cleared until 1979 to make way for a timber yard and saw-mill[27].

8

A RETROSPECT

At the time of writing, there has been no mining in the Wyre Forest Coalfield for a quarter of a century. In all probability, this is the longest period of inactivity since the sixteenth century. The cessation of mining has been met with mixed reactions

The closure of Alveley Colliery was received with much local bitterness and there was a strong feeling that natural justice had not been done. However, with the changes that were taking place nationally to the coal industry, it would never have been in a strong position. Had it survived, it would almost certainly have gone in the closures of the 1980s, when replacement jobs were much harder to come by. The events of 1968-1969 were probably a merciful release. Even at the time there were those in the village who were not particularly sorry to see the end of underground work. For a long period, little was done to mark the mining industry. The surviving colliery buildings were converted into an industrial estate and in 1986 the tips at Highley and Alveley were made into a country park. As the twenty-fifth anniversary of closure came closer, pressure grew to mark the event and commemorate the area's mining past. Consequently a memorial to the local miners based on a colliery-winding wheel was unveiled in 1994 on the site of Highley Colliery by Ray Hasbury, the former manager during the 1950s. On the same day, the local carnival included a reunion of ex-miners followed by a miner's service in church. While inevitably the numbers of ex-miners are now rapidly decreasing, there is much more awareness of the contribution of coal mining.

At Bayton there was less ill-feeling surrounding closure of the mine; many thought that the pit had done well to survive as long as it had. Employing far fewer men than at Alveley, the industry in its final years had only a minimal impact and it seems largely to have been forgotten, except by a few. Unlike at Highley, where there have been proposals for fresh mining, both opencast and latterly underground, that have attracted controversy.

What are the prospects for future mining in the coalfield? There certainly remain significant reserves of coal. The area which has most recently seen a proposal for renewed mining is to the south of Hunthouse Wood, extending into areas left untouched by the Mole Brothers' mine. There have been plans to sink

Highley Colliery Surveyors, 1916. John Staley, Trevor Stonehouse and Horace Lloyd on their way to Kinlet Colliery to carry out the quarterly surveys of the workings. Horace Lloyd was a fine musician and a founder member of Highley Brass Band. He wrote a march for the band entitled The Highlean *and collaborated with Sir Edward Elgar on the writing of brass band music.*

a drift and work the coal by pillar-and-stall. Here and elsewhere in the south of the coalfield there remain untouched areas in the Old Hall Bats, Main Sulphur and Hard Mine which could form the basis of a relatively low-cost operation, if conditions were appropriate. In the north of the coalfield, the vast majority of the proposed Alveley take to the east of the Romsley Fault remains unworked. Of course, the geological problems that afflicted Alveley would probably recur and it is perhaps doubtful whether large-scale investment would be worthwhile. Nonetheless, the coal might be tempting at some time in the future. Elsewhere in the area there are likely to be reserves in the vicinity of Kinlet and Billingsley, but again these would probably be difficult to mine due to the geology. Whether the Wyre Forest Coalfield ever again sees activity ultimately depends not on local factors, but on national considerations and the place of coal in the economy. If it is seen as a valuable fuel, at some point it may be worth sinking new pits; if it is regarded as a throwback to the past along with charcoal and wood faggots, then the areas will probably remain undisturbed.

Regardless of the future of coal production, the remains of past mining are extensive and impressive. In rural areas, derelict mining sites were often left undisturbed. With the rapid rundown of the British coal industry since the 1980s,

Surface workers at the pit top, Kinlet, 1933. Left to right: O. Betteridge, E. Brick, -?-, E. Shaw, G. Hunt (banksman).

these remains are now assuming increasing importance as examples of an industry that has elsewhere been almost totally obliterated. At the moment it is possible to view artefacts ranging from medieval bell-pits through to a Victorian winding house and a range of surface buildings from the 1950s. Indeed, whole landscapes can still be found that have been fashioned by mining and miners; the pits, transport routes and the miners houses, smallholdings and settlements. However, virtually none of the former mining sites have any kind of protection. Since the 1930s, probably a third to a half of existing sites have been damaged or destroyed. Little has been properly recorded or investigated. Clearly it is not feasible or even desirable to preserve everything, but it is to be hoped that sufficient of the remaining sites will gain recognition and survive to give future generations an insight into the mining industry of the Wyre Forest Coalfield.

Notes

The following abbreviations have been used throughout:

BGS; British Geological Survey
BJ; *Bridgnorth Journal*
BWJ; *Berrow's Worcester Journal*
KT; *Kidderminster Times*
PRO; Public Record Office
SC; *Shrewsbury Chronicle*
SRRO; Shropshire Records and Research Office
StRO; Staffordshire Record Office
TSAS; *Transaction of the Shropshire Archaeological Society*
WRO; Worcestershire Record Office. References for the WRO show the bulk accession (BA) number.

Chapter 1

1) Unless otherwise stated, this chapter is based on the 1:50,000 Series BGS maps 167 and 182, and their accompanying memoirs; *The Geology of the Country around Droitwich, Abberley and Kidderminster*, G.H. Mitchell, R.W. Pocock and J.H. Taylor, HMSO, 1962 and *Bridgnorth and Dudley*, T.H. Whitehead and R.W. Pocock, HMSO, 1947.
2) J. Randall, *Mining Journal*, June 1869, 447; R.I. Murchison, *The Silurian System*, 131-140, London, 1839.
3) J. Phillips, *The Malvern Hills compared with Abberley, Memoirs of the Geological Survey*, Part 2, 1848.
4) Murchison, *op. cit.* See also Murchison's notebooks in the library of the Geological Society, Burlington House, London.
5) D. Jones, *The structure of the Wyre Forest Coalfield*, Trans. Fed. Inst. Min. Eng., **7**, 287-301, 577-580, 1894: T.C. Cantrilll, *A Contribution to the Geology of the Wyre Forest Coalfield*, Kidderminster, 1895. Notes of Jones and Cantrill are held by the BGS at Keyworth, Notts, in the National Geosciences Databank and the library, respectively.

Chapter 2

1) R.C. Gaut, *A History of Worcestershire Agriculture and Rural Evolution*, 45, Littlebury & Co., Worcester, 1939.
2) PRO SP12 Vol. 36, No.1, *Survey of Earnwood*, 1565.
3) D. Chapman, *Cleobury Park Furnace*, Cleobury Chronicles, **4**, 56-65, 1996: D.R. Poyner, *Early ironworking at Chorley*, Cleobury Chronicles, **5**, 1998: Pocock & Whitehead, *op. cit.*, 49: Crump ms, Jones Papers, BGS.
4) A.D. Dyer, *The City of Worcester in the Sixteenth Century*, Leicester University Press, 1973: J. Randall, *Industry in Shropshire*, 450, in *The Victoria County History of Shropshire*; Vol. 1, Ed. R. Page, Archibald Constable, London, 1909.
5) T.C. Purton, *Some account of the manor of Chetton*, TSAS, 2nd Series **6**, 177-190, 1894.
6) J. Hatcher, *History of the British Coal Industry* **1**, Clarendon, Oxford, 1993.
7) Hatcher, *op. cit.*, 146 *et seq.*.
8) Crump Ms, Jones Papers, BGS, BWJ 24/9/1853.
9) C. Hadfield, *Canals of South Wales and the Borders*, 191-3, David & Charles, Newton Abbot, 1967: I. Cohen, *The Kington and Stourport Canal*, Trans. Woolhope Naturalists Field Club, **35**, 267 *et seq.*, 1957.
10) Figures based on 1851 census. In the *Mining Journal*, 3 December 1870, Daniel Jones estimated output as 15,000 tons pa.
11) Jones Papers, BGS.
12) Letter to *Mining Journal*, July 1869, 494.
13) Men estimated from Mineral Statistics/List of coal mines, HMSO, various years. Output estimated from Colliery Yearbook, various years.
14) The working methods are largely based on accounts given by ex-miners employed at the pits of the Highley Mining Company as detailed in the references to chapter 5, or by the late Messrs T.H. Stonehouse and G. Bramall.
15) Mineral statistics, 1896.
16) Arley Parish Registers, Worcestershire Parish Register Society, **4**, 1915.
17)) StRO, QS/R (transcript) Box 3 roll 76 No. 21, quoted in P.M. Frost, *Growth and Localization of Rural Industry in South Staffordshire 1560-1720*, Birmingham University Ph.D.: Nottingham University Library, Middleton Manuscripts, 177/37-38.
18) G. Nair, *Highley; the development of a community*, Blackwell, Oxford, 1988; G. Nair & D. Poyner, *The Coming of Coal: Industrial Development in a South Shropshire Parish*, 87-103, Midland History, **18**, 1993.
19) Chelmarsh, Neenton and Billingsley Parish Registers, Shropshire Parish Register Society, **iii**, 1903: Census data; summary tables, various years: British Library, Add. Mss. 21018, undated copy of notes by Rev. J. Plymley.
20) Probable miners were identified from the Highley and Billingsley parish registers, supplemented by the Highley Easter Books (see Nair & Poyner, *op. cit.* for details of this source) and these were used to search the International Genealogical Index for Shropshire, Worcestershire, Staffordshire, Lancashire and Northumberland.
21) Reports of HM Inspectors of Mines.
22) Information ex-Mr B. Crowther, BEM; *Coal Magazine*, various years.
23) House of Commons Papers 1803-4, XIII, 420, Abstracts of returns relative to the expense and maintenance of the poor; *Worcester Herald* 5/6/1851; BWJ 30/8/1856, 9/11/1867; BJ 17/3/1888.
24) KT 28/1/1882.
25) Information ex-Messrs L. Giles and. J. Jones; *Bridgnorth Journal*, various dates, 1888-1914.
26) Notebook of Noah Lawton, c/o Mrs M. Price, Highley; notes by T.H. Stonehouse, authors' collection: information and collections of Messrs L. Giles and F. Jones; KT 27 September 1930.
27) Information ex-Messrs J. Jones, F. Jones, L. Giles, Mrs. E. Deakin; Diaries, authors' collection; KT 6/1/1912.
28) Info ex-Messrs G.W. Poyner, C. Hepplewhite; Kelly's Post Office Directory for Highley, various years.

29) Info ex-Mrs E.M. Poyner, Mrs E. Deakin.
30) Poyner & Nair, *op. cit.*.
31) H.G. Macnab, A letter to J. Whitmore..., V. Griffiths, London, 1801.
32) BWJ 2/3/1878, 22/8/1850, 2/1/1875; BJ 30/7/1859.
33) BWJ 13/3/1875, 7/10/1854.
34) The date of 1883 is quoted by R. Page-Arnott, *The Miners*, **1**, 1949. For the career of Winwood see Bellamy and Saville, *Dictionary of Labour Bibliography*, **2**, 410-13.
35) Minute Book, Highley Mining Company, Library, Ironbridge Institute for Industrial Archaeology, Coalbrookdale
36) SC 14/10/1887; BJ 29/10/1887, 21/4/1888.
37) Board of Trade, Report on strikes and lockouts of 1894, Parliamentary Papers 1895.XCII.
38) BJ 26/7/1903
39) Diary, authors' collection
40) BJ 9/3/1912; KT 2/3/1912, 16/3/1912; Diary, authors' collection; info ex-Mr W. Poundford.
41) BJ 25/5/1912, 1/6/1912, 30/1/1915, 27/2/1915.
42) KT 4/9/1920, 23/10/1920, 6/11/1920.
43) BJ 16/6/1921, 5/11/1921; KT 31/3/1921, 7/4/1921, 26/5/1921, 18/6/1921/ 25/6/1921, 6/5/1922; Info ex-Messrs J. Jones, L.Giles, G. Davies.
44) KT 3/2/1923, 4/8/1923; 7/5/1926, 22/5/1926, 29/5/1926, 5/6/1926, 19/6/1926; Info ex-Messr J. Jones, J. Mantle, L. Giles, G. Davies.
45) Minutes of the Highley and Kinlet Miners Association, c/o Mr. G.N. Davies, Highley.
46) *ibid*.
47) *ibid*.
48) Register of Members, Bayton Lodge, East Worcs. and South Staffs. Miners Association, authors' collection; KT 11/11/1949.

17) BWJ 28/5/1772, 18/4/1805: SRRO 1045/27: Kinlet parish registers, 1809 Glebe Terrier, 63.
18) HMSO, Dept of Mines, list of coal mines; Abandonment Plan, Winwoods Colliery, Coal Authority Mining Records Office, Bretby, Staffs.
19) S. Shaw, History of Staffordshire, **ii**, 253, 1801: WRO 10863/33.
20) W. Scott, *Stourbridge and its vicinity*, 479, 1832: Pocock & Whitehead, *op.cit.*, 57: BWJ 13/3/1834.
21) PRO BT 41/628/3421 Shatterford Coal & Iron Mining Company (see also BWJ 11/3/1847 for prospectus): BT 41/25/29 Arley Coal & Iron Mining, Brick, Lime & Coke Company; BT 31/311/1078 Arley Mining Company: WRO 4000/161, 10863/33.
22) PRO BT/31/239/1078 Arley Pottery and Firebrick Company: R Hunt, Mineral Statistics, *op.cit.*, list of brickworks, 1858: T.C. Cantrilll, No 8 Notebook, BGS.
23) J.M. Fellows, *Sinkings and borings at Arley Colliery, Shatterford, near Bewdley*, Trans. S. Staffs. East Worcs. Min. Eng., **6**, 39-42, 1880: G.E. Roberts, *Deep sinking for coal in the Wyre Forest Coalfield*, Geologist, 421-6, 468, 1861: E. Lees, *Rocks of the Shatterford District*, Proc. Dudley Midland Geol. Soc., 13-14, 1891/2: H.R. Mayo, *Annals of Arley*, 90, Kidderminster, Wm Hepworth, 1914: BWJ 17/11/1860, 24/5/1861.
24) WRO 10863/33, 4000/161: T.C. Cantrill, No 8 notebook, *op. cit.*.
25) Mineral Statistics *op. cit.*, Colliery Yearbook *op. cit.*: OS 6":1 mile 3rd Series Map, NW Worcs, Arley and Shatterford: Info ex-Messrs W. Westwood, J. Mantle: KT Jan 1936.
26) BWJ 22/4/1824: Pocock & Whitehead, *op.cit.*, 57.
27) N.M. Barrett, *Portrait of Dowles*, 23-25, Bewdley, 1974: KT 17/3/1924, Dowles.
28) S. Davies, *Rural Colliers of Wyre*, 84-98, Folk Life, **22**, 1983/4.
29) Jones papers, *op. cit.*, Cantrill notebook, *op.cit.*

Chapter 3

1) T.C. Purton *Some account of the manor of Chetton*, TSAS, 2nd Series **6**, 177-190, 1894.
2) BWJ June 20th 1816: SRRO QR238/78, Inquest on John Tompkis, 31st Jan 1809: R. Baugh, Map of Shropshire: OS Preliminary Drawing 213, 1814 (located in Birmingham Reference Library, 661185/23).
3) BJ 8/11/1856, 16/1/1858, 30/7/59, 5/9/1863, 12/3/1864, 22/12/1866, 14/3/1868, 15/5/1869: D. Jones, *Spirobis Limestone in the Forest of Wyre Coalfield*, 1870, privately published: Jones Papers, BGS.
4) *Eddowes Shropshire Journal* 21/2/1851: BJ 15/5/1856, 29/10/1859, 30/5/1863: SC 23/8/1861.
5) Pocock & Whitehead, *op. cit.*, 74: BJ 15/3/1856: Jones Papers, BGS.
6) *Eddowes Shropshire Journal* 5/3/1851: BJ 27/8/59, 6/6/1858, 16/5/1863: SRRO 1396 1396/4,6,8,20,24,34,40.
7) SRRO 1224/163.
8) Chelmarsh, Neenton and Billingsley Parish Registers, Shropshire Parish Register Society, **iii**, 1903: SC July 3rd 1812: BWJ Aug 13th 1818.
9) For a detailed account of Stanley and references, see Nair and Poyner, *op. cit.*. We are grateful to Dr Stafford Lindsay, Newcastle University, for information on Benjamin Thompson.
10) Kinlet Parish Registers, **viii**, Shropshire Parish Register Society, 1917.
11) Arley Parish Registers, Worcestershire Parish Register Society, **4**, 1915.
12) Nottingham University Library, Middleton Manuscripts, 177/37-38: SRRO 1047/88.
13) B. Trinder, *The Industrial Revolution in Shropshire*, Phillimore, 1973: R.S. Smith, *Early Coal Mining around Nottingham 1500-1650*, 66-80, Nottingham University Press, 1989: M.J.T. Lewis, *Early Wooden Railways*, Routledge & Kegan Paul, London, 1974.
14) StRO, QS/R (transcript) Box 3 roll 76 No. 21, quoted in P.M. Frost, *Growth and Localization of Rural Industry in South Staffordshire 1560-1720*, Birmingham University Ph.D.
15) SRRO 3320 Cleobury Court Baron rolls, survey of Earnwood, 1643: PRO E134 /1648/9 /Hil 2.
16) SRRO 3320/18B/7

Chapter 4

1) Pocock & Whitehead, *op. cit.*, 49: Crump Ms, Jones Papers, BGS. See also note 3 of chapter 2.
2) R.A.Lewis, *Two Partnerships of the Knights-A Study of the Midland Iron Industry in the eighteenth century*, 70-2, MA Thesis, Birmingham University, 1949: Knight Ms (WRO), General account of the Bringewood partnership, 244-265.
3) Jean Roque, Map of Shropshire, 1754.
4) Crump ms., *op. cit.*.
5) *ibid*.
6) *ibid*.
7) *ibid*.
8) *ibid*.
9) *ibid*.
10) SRRO 3320: Pocock & Whitehead *op. cit.*: *Structure of the Wyre Forest Coalfield*, D. Jones, *op. cit.*: Info ex-Mr. W. Tolley.
11) BWJ 21/5/1789, 13/1/1831; SRRO Inquest on Thomas Winwood, 8th July 1778.
12) Kinlet Estate Account ledgers (held at Kinlet Hall, Shrops.,), various years.
13) Mineral Statistics, *op. cit.*: KT 25/12/1925, Info ex-Mr. G. Davies.
14) Mineral Statistics, *op. cit.*: Colliery Yearbook, various years: BJ 16, 23/3/1935: Info ex-Messrs H. Bache, B. Crowther: Pocock & Whitehead, *op. cit.*, 49: Colliery Guardian, 15/2/1935.

Chapter 5

1) Most of the history of Billingsley is to be found in the following PRO files; C13/36/20, C13/615/20, C13/2835, C13/2413, C13/2403, C13/2408. See also N. Mutton, *Forgotten Industries of Billingsley*, 29, Shropshire Magazine, 1971, and *Billingsley Furnace, a Phenomenon of the French Wars*, typescript, SRRO, 1966/6. Further details are in R. Nair & D. Poyner, *The Coming of Coal: Industrial Development in a South Shropshire Parish*, 87-103, Midland History, **18**, 1993.
2) Correspondence and papers of William Childe, authors' collection.
3) Crump ms, *op. cit.*
4) Christ Church College, Oxford, Archives, MS Estates 84/143-170.

5) Mutton, *op. cit.* and *The forges at Eardington and Hampton Loade*, 235-243, Trans. Shrops. Arch. Soc., **58**, 1967-8: PRO C13/1883/21: SRRO 6000/688, 81/234-7; SC 26/6/1812; BWJ 12/3/1812, 14/5/1812, 11/6/1812, 21/1/1813, 9/9/1813.
6) Mutton typescript, *op. cit.*: *Eddowes Shropshire Journal* 5/1/1814: SC 17/8/1817: PRO C13/36/20.
7) HM Inspectors of Mines reports, Shropshire, 1868: D. Jones, letters to Mining Journal, 31 December 1870 and Geol. Mag, Feb. 1873: Jones papers, BGS, *op. cit.*: Sale notice, Billingsley Colliery, 1874, Johnson, Poole and Bloomer Archive, Dudley: BWJ 22/5/1875: PRO BT31/2081/9268.
8) Plan of Billingsley Colliery, 1877, Johnson, Poole and Bloomer Archive, Dudley: SRRO, Lease of Billingsley Colliery, 1877: PRO BT 31/2081/9268: BWJ 6/1/1877: KT 11/1/1879.
9) BT 31/208/9268: BWJ 30/10/1879. The earthworks for the railway line were completed as far as New England, on the Kinlet-Billingsley parish boundary before work stopped. They are recorded on both the first and second series OS 1;2500 maps of this area (1882 and 1901). They were eventually incorporated into a railway built in 1911/12 (details below).
10) SC 21/1/1881.
11) PRO BT 31/2814/15423, BT 31/2971/16688: BWJ 28/5/1881, 10/6/1882, 12/5/1883, 30/6/1883, 21/7/1883, 11/8/1883.
12) BWJ 12/5/1881, 21/7/1883.
13) W. Molyneux, *On the Highley Colliery*, Mining Journal, Nov. 15th 1879: Minute Book, Highley Mining Company, Library, Ironbridge Institute for Industrial Archaeology, Coalbrookdale: Notebook of Noah Lawton, c/o Mrs. M. Price, Highley.
14) Minute Book, HMCo, *op. cit.*: StRO D876, Register of Members of the Highley Mining Company: SC 14/10/1887.
15) Mineral Statistics, 1892 *et seq.*, *op. cit.*: Noah Lawton's Notebook, *op.cit.*: BJ 19/1/1894: E. Wain, Report on Kinlet Colliery, 25th July 1905, authors' collection, Info ex-Mr. A. Breakwell.
16) Info ex-Mr J. Jones: Marcy Hemingway, Abstract of Mineral Leases on the Kinlet Estate, 1919, c/o David Postle, Kidderminster Railway Museum: BJ 19/1/1901.
17) Mineral statistics, *op. cit.*, Alveley Colliery, NCB Information Sheet, n.d.
18) W. Smith and K. Beddoes, *The Cleobury Mortimer and Ditton Priors Light Railway*, pp 18, 23, 35, 111, Oxford Publishing Company, Oxford, 1990: PRO BT31 19547/110525: Stock Exchange Year Book, Stock Exchange Official Information Book, 1910-17.
19) Info ex-Mr. J. Jones.
20) SRRO 119/42
21) BJ 14/2/1914, 7/3/1914.
22) Derricutt papers and diaries, authors' collection: PRO MT 2180/6: BJ 13/9/1921.
23) BJ 20/1/1912, 9/3/1912, 27/7/1912, 17/8/1912.
24) BJ 27/2/1913, 6/6/1914: KT 17/10/1914: PRO BT31 19547/110525: Mineral Statistics, *op. cit.*: Info ex-Mr. J. Jones: Report W. Meachem, 1915, authors' collection.
25) Info ex-Mr. J. Jones: SRRO 119/42
26) Mineral Statistics, *op. cit.*: NCB Information Sheet, Alveley Colliery, nd: PRO COAL 34/405.
27) Info ex-Messrs J. Jones, L. Giles, G. Davies.
28) Mineral Statistics, *op. cit.*: NCB Information Sheet, Alveley Colliery, nd: BJ 28/11/1921: Letter H. Foster to H.M. Co, authors' collection: Info ex-Messrs G. Davies, C. Hepplewhite.
29) Info ex-Messrs J. Jones, H. Bache, B. Crowther.
30) Info ex-Messrs J. Jones, B. Crowther: Notes on interview between H.M.Co. and R.W. Pocock, 1/12/1931, authors' collection.
31) BJ 20/8/1935.
32) Info ex-Messrs J. Jones, B. Crowther: Letter H. Stonehouse to GWR, 1940, collection of David Postle.
33) PRO COAL 34/405, COAL 38/376.
34) Mineral Statistics, *op. cit.*: Info ex-Messrs J. Jones, H. Bache, B. Crowther.
35) PRO COAL 34/405, POWE 42/7, 42/20: BJ 5/1/1947: *Guide to the Collieries* (published by the Colliery Guardian), various years.
36) Pit profile, Highley, Coal magazine, Feb 1954, 10-11: Guide to the Collieries, *op cit.*
37) BJ 10/6/1960, 8/5/1967; HM Inspectors of Mines Report, West Midlands Division, 1955.
38) BJ 8/5/1967: Abandonment Plan, Alveley Colliery, info ex-Mr R.O. Hemsley.
39) Guide to the Collieries, *op. cit.*
40) BJ 8/5/1967
41) Colliery Consultative Committee Minutes, 15/11/1967; 7/3, 13/5, 28/5, 5/11, 19/11, 4/12/1968: Correspondence Jasper Moore, Wilfred Mirron and George Davies, 1967-8: Minutes, Highley Branch, NUM, 1967-69, c/o Mr G.N. Davies, Highley.

Chapter 6.

1) A.D. Dyer, *The City of Worcester in the Sixteenth Century*, Leicester University Press, 1973: J. Randall, *Industry in Shropshire*, 450, in The Victoria County History of Shropshire; Vol. 1, Ed. R. Page, Archibald Constable, London, 1909.
2) J. Noake, *The Monastery and Cathedral of Worcester*, 519-20, Longmore, Worcester, 1866: Parliamentary Survey of Worcestershire, 1649-51.
3) Noake, *The Monastery and Cathedral of Worcester*, *op. cit.*, 519-20: PRO E134/18Geo2/Mich 10: Maxwell Fraser, *Companion into Worcestershire*, 11-12, Methuen, London, 1939: BWJ 17/5/1759.
4) WRO 2309/53: BWJ 29/6/1797, 27/3/1783, 5/5/1785, 16/2/1792, 23/3/1797, 26/11/1807, 11/6/1840.
5) BWJ 5/10/1786, 27/3/1783, 12/5/1785, 5/12/1833: R. Baugh, Map of Worcestershire, 1808.
6) BWJ 5/4/1792; Birmingham Reference Library Ms 467145.
7) WRO 2309/53: BWJ 7/3/1805, 8/5/1806, 5/6/1806. (The WRO papers are among those that deal with the Brown family estates at Old Hall, and it is assumed that these are also the estates involved with the Pensax Coal and Iron Company. However, the correspondence dealing with the PCICo. is addressed to a Mrs Browning.)
8) Hadfield, *op. cit.*: OS First Series preliminary drawing 214: BWJ 17/2/1848, 4/5/1848. The Railway and Canal Historical Society produced a map of the Leominster Canal in 1967 showing three branches to the Pensax tramway. However, the western branch leads nowhere and there is no field evidence to suggest that it ever existed. It is also not shown by the Ordnance Survey.
9) Trade directories, various years. BRL 467145: WRO 268/3967: Noake, *The Monastery and Cathedral of Worcester*, *op. cit.*, 520: BWJ, 29/12/1866, 22/6/1867, 2/1/1874, 27/11/1874, 3/3/1875.
10) Davies, Rural Colliers of Wyre, *op. cit.*: Birmingham Reference Library 399102-3.
11) BWJ 23/2/1815, 31/5/1821, 8/3/1825.
12) Mineral Statistics, *op.cit.*: Plans, authors' collection: Jones papers, BGS.
13) WRO 4600/765: BWJ 20/8/1864.
14) WRO 4600/452: HM Inspectors of Mines reports: BWJ 30/10/1880, 11/8/1883, 26/12/1885.
15) WRO 4600/452, 454, 85v: BWJ 23/11/1895: Field trip to Mamble, Trans. Worcs. Nat. Club, 1908.
16) Mineral Statistics: Plans, Bramall papers: Mitchell, Pocock and Taylor, 79, *op. cit.*: Info ex-Mr. W. Giles.
17) BWJ 30/10/1777, 5/5/1785; Isaac Taylor, Map of Worcestershire, 1772.
18) Mineral Statistics, *op. cit.* and trade directories.
19) Census returns: Minerals statistics, *op. cit.*: KT 19/4/1913 Biographical note on Septimus Dudley: BWJ 30/6/1865: BJ 27/4/1867: WRO 4600/831.
20) BWJ 27/10/1855, 8/8/1857, 30/6/1866: J. Noake, *Guide to Worcestershire*, Longman, Worcester, 1868.
21) WRO 4600/831: BWJ 14/5/1881, 16/7/1881, 21/12/1895: Mineral Statistics, *op. cit.*: HM Inspectors of Mines Reports, *op. cit.*.
22) *Worcester Herald*, 3/7/1851: BWJ 8/1/1881, 16/7/1881, 12/8/1882: HM Inspectors of Mines reports, WRO4600/13iv.
23) R.D. Thompson, *Rock*, 16, Kenneth Tomkinson Ltd., Kidderminster, 1981: KT 12/7/1870: WRO 7930: PRO BT31/5826/40884.
24) Prospectuses and reports, authors' collection: HM Inspectors of Mines reports: Mitchell, Pocock & Whitehead, *op. cit.*, 78: Jones

papers, BGS: BWJ 13/8/1898.
25) Mineral Statistics, *op. cit.*
26) Bramall papers, authors collection.
27) Noake, Guide to Worcs, *op. cit.*, 252.
28) BWJ 27/2/1875: BJ 28/8/1910: L. Richardson, *Wells and Springs of Worcestershire*, 96-7, Memoirs Geol. Survey, 1930: Jones Papers, BGS; Report, Daniel Jones to Captain Childe 1896, Johnson, Poole and Bloomer Archive, Dudley.
29) Report on Underground Trials in Coal Gasification, HMSO, London, 1956.
30) PRO COAL 30/36: R.D. Thompson, *Rock*, Tomkinson, Kidderminster, 1981.

24) PRO COAL 34/59: Record of sinkings, record of output, Bramall papers, authors' collection.
25) Bayton Col. Co., Annual report, 1948, authors' collection.
26) Letter to R.W. Pocock, nd, Bramall papers, authors' collection: KT 4/11/1949, 11/11/1949, 3/2/1950, 21/4/1950.
27) Plans, authors' collection: I.J. Brown, *The Mines of Shropshire*, Moorland, Derbyshire, 1976: Info ex-Mr. H. Jenkins, KT 1/6/1979.

Chapter 7

1) WRO 5278/15, 6442/1, 305/1 (Enrolment of Papist Estates, **2**, Lands of Edward Blount).
2) BWJ 30/10/1777, 28/3/1822, Prattinton Mss **1**, 61 (Society of Antiquities, London): WRO 6442/3: OS 2":1 mile preliminary drawing 206E, 1817.
3) C. Hadfield, *Canals of South Wales and the Borders*, 191-3, David & Charles, Newton Abbot, 1967: I. Cohen, *The Kington and Stourport Canal*, Trans. Woolhope Naturalists Field Club, **35**, 267 *et seq.*, 1957.
4) Humberside County Record Office, Beverley, DDCC/147/35-77.
5) OS 2in:1 mile preliminary drawing 206E, 1817; Mamble tithe map, 1840, WRO; 1st Series OS map, 1:5000, 1881/2.
6) Murchisson notebook, M/N67, *op. cit*
7) Jones papers, BGS, *op. cit.*.
8) Hunt, Mineral Statistics, 1854 *et seq.*, PRO COAL 34/59: Bramall papers, authors collection
9) KT 23/2/1922.
10) BWJ 2/8/1832: WRO 6442/3: OS 2in:1 mile preliminary drawing 206E, 1817.
11) Mineral Statistics, *op. cit.*: WRO 4600/502ii, 4600/476; HM Inspectors of Mines Reports, S.Staffs and East Worcs., Parliamentary Papers, HMSO, 1860.
12) WRO 4600/157, 4600/670
13) BT 31/9679/71978: Bramall papers, *op. cit.*.
14) Lease, Wickstead to Smallshaw, 1904, authors' collection: OS 1:2500 maps, Bayton, 1st and 2nd series (1882 and 1902) show the development of mining in Bayton at this period. For the aerial ropeway, see K. Beddoes and W.H. Smith, The Tenbury and Bewdley Railway, 64-5, Wild Swan Publications, Didcot, 1995. We cannot be certain that we have correctly identified Smallshaw as the sinker of Bayton No 1 as it is possible that it was started by Viggars and the Bayton Coal and Brick Company. In this case the small working close to Bayton Village which we have postulated to be the work of the former must be an older working on the Shakenhurst estate.
15) Beddoes and Smith, *op. cit.*, 70-3, 81: Mineral Statistics, *op. cit.*: Directory of Directors, 1914: Sale agreement, Smallshaw to Whitworth Wright, 1911; Agreements, GWR and Bayton Col. Co., 1911, 1912; Stock of the Bayton Col. Co., 1914, all authors' collection.
16) KT 31/7/1915, 8/1/1916, 8/7/1916, 15/7/1916: Agreement, purchase of Bayton Colliery, 1914; leases, 1916; G. Bramall, A brief history of the company, nd, unpublished, all authors' collection.
17) G. Bramall, Brief history, *op. cit.*, Inventory of Bayton Colliery, nd, Balance Sheet, Bayton Col. Co., June 1923, all authors' collection.
18) Notes, G. Bramall, authors' collection.
19) PRO COAL 38/62: Bramall papers, *op. cit.*: Mineral Statistics, *op. cit.*.
20) Leases and correspondence, Old Hall Colliery, 1929-31, Shakenhurst Estate Minerals, Bramall papers.
21) Notes, G. Bramall, authors' collection; Record of sinkings, Notes on colliery workings on the Abberley Estate, all Bramall papers, authors' collection.
22) *Ibid*
23) *Ibid*: G. Bramall, Drifts, 1944, nd, unpublished, authors' collection.

Appendix I: Gazetteer

Where grid references are not supplied, these may be found in Appendix 2; List of Mines. Most of these sites are on private land; inclusion in this gazetteer does not imply right of access!

Abberley
The remains at Poolhouse are largely ploughed out, although several shafts can still be identified by faint earthworks. At Beehive, the eastern complex survives only as soil marks visible after ploughing. The spoil tips of Nos 3, 4 and 5 are still extant. The best remains are those of Fieldbrook. The edge of the clay pit for the brickworks can be made out. No.2 shaft has a concrete cap and there is still a low spoil mound next to No.3 shaft. In the woods, the brick ring of No.4 still remains, next to a concrete wall, presumably part of the winding house (SO745679).

Alveley
The extensive spoil tips of Alveley Colliery form part of the Severn Valley Country Park (SO757838). The Country Park Visitor Centre has a collection of photographs and artefacts from the mine. The pithead baths, lamproom, canteen, deployment centre and weighbridge survive unaltered as part of the industrial estate. The colliery offices also survive, albeit in an altered condition. The tramway leading to the screens on the Highley side of the river is now a footpath; odd lengths of rail and a return wheel are visible. The bridge over the Severn is still present at the time of writing (2000) although it is scheduled for replacement. It is to be hoped that a portion of this historic structure can be preserved. The aerial ropeway that replaced the tramway has also left traces; the bases of pylons either side of the bridge are visible and some of the guide rope still hangs from the trees. There are also foundations of the angle station on the Highley side of the river. The site of the screens is now a picnic area and the Country Park Halt on the Severn Valley Railway; however, traces of sleepers from the old colliery sidings can be found in situ. The lagoon built to take the slurry from the washery survives and there are the remains of several tubs in the undergrowth.

Areley Kings
Gladder Brook drift remains open in Areley Wood.

Bayton
There are significant spoil tips at the sites of the Shakenhurst pits, Mill Colliery and Bayton No.1. The bases of the aerial ropeway are also visible.

Billingsley
The oldest remains in Billingsley are found in the Deserts Wood. Substantial slag heaps and a dam mark the remains of a bloomery of probable late medieval date (SO706840). The very many shafts that surround this must date from medieval times to the start of the nineteenth century. There are several drainage levels close to the brook and possible wheel pits; suggestions of a once sophisticated drainage system. Many of the tracks throughout the wood must also have been associated with the mines. On the brow of the bank are the early nineteenth century workings associated with Johnson & Co. There are a number of possible engine house sites and in the surrounding fields are spoil tips and probable gin circles. At Billingsley blast furnace there survives an engine house, a few retaining walls and a (now dry) pool (SO714840). It is possible to trace the tramway that led to the Severn at Highley. At New England there is a good section of the rope-worked incline (SO724838); by the mines themselves there are rather more confusing earthworks

(SO710837).

Behind the Cape of Good Hope Inn (itself probably contemporary with the workings of Johnson & Co.) is the site of the later Billingsley Colliery. Although a ruined office block dates from the early days of the mine in the 1870s, most of the buildings date from 1910-1912. These include the main offices, lamproom, fitter's shop, blacksmith's shop and a garage. Close by are the houses built for the manager and undermanager. It is possible to follow the line of the tramway down from the mine to the site of the screens at Prior's Moor where some foundations and earthworks remain (SO716835). The line of the railway to the Severn Valley in Kinlet is largely intact and most of it is a public footpath. Various bridges and a weighbridge remain. At Prior's Moor there are also foundations of cottages probably built in around 1800 for the earlier phase of mining.

A shaft can be found north of Billingsley Hall Farm, probably a mid-nineteenth century trial (SO712860).

Chelmarsh
A shaft is still open in Whitcombs Wood (SO743852). By Dinney Farm there is a large spoil tip dating from the mine of around 1880 (SO717869).

Chetton
Faint traces of spoil tips and shafts at Eudon (SO686895).

Eardington
Spoil tips and shaft depressions.

Highley
There are traces of shafts and workings alongside the Borle Brook for much of its length. The late eighteenth century tramway that led to Billingsley is well preserved for much of its length and at Brooksmouth Wharf, MacNab's house still stands, although the clerk's house is currently in ruins (SO753817). There are also the foundations of colliers' houses at New England that date from this period (SO726838).

There are a few earthworks marking the site of Stanley Colliery; these probably include a short length of tramway, a shaft and the base of an engine house. Near to the river is a large spoil tip and there are traces of workmen's cottages along the riverbank. The Ship Inn, once owned by the colliery proprietors, is still in business.

The site of the Highley Colliery has been turned into part of the Severn Valley Park. The incline that leads from the mine to the Severn Valley Railway is still present, as is the site of the colliery sidings. The colliery office has been converted into housing. A modern mine wheel has been erected on the site as a memorial to the local miners. Close to the river, the colliery pump house also survives (SO750831).

The centre of Highley village is an excellent example of a mining settlement. The oldest terrace is Silverdale, built in around 1885, originally called Providence Terrace. Coronation Street, Barke Street (named after a director of the Highley Mining Company) and Orchard Street were erected at the turn of the century; the rather more genteel Church Street dates from 1911-1912. Most of the shops, the chapel and the Working Men's Club were built from 1900-1914. In the centre of the village the Miners Welfare Fund built the recreation ground and village hall in the 1930s. Clee View, a long brick terrace, was built in 1911-1912 by the rival Billingsley Colliery Company, who started work on Garden Village in 1914. The First World War meant that this elegant development was never completed.

Kinlet
By the Birch Farm is a spoil tip of *c.*1800 (SO736808) and there are more extensive remains of shafts and spoil tips either side of the road at Brook's Coppice. Spoil tips are also present at Kingswood farm. At Winwoods farm the site of the 1920s mine is still visible.

By far the most impressive remains in Kinlet are those of the Highley Mining Company's mine.

The large, roofless engine house of 1894 dominates the site. Foundations remain of the fan house, a second winding engine, boilers, workshops, screens and the locomotive shed. The shafts have been capped with concrete. The line of railway leading to the Severn Valley Railway is still intact.

Kinver
Spoils tips mark the site of the nineteenth century Compton sinking.

Mamble
At the Mamble colliery itself there are a well-preserved series of spoil tips, shafts, tramways and other earthworks stretching from Footrid Cottage (SO680708) to beyond Soddington Hall (SO695811). The earliest probably date from the end of the eighteenth century and progress chronologically eastwards to the final workings of 1924 by the hall. The site of the 'footrid', a drainage level, is marked by a spring discharging iron-impregnated water into the Marl Brook (SO678807). It is possible to trace the line of the tramway from the mines to Southnett Wharf at the start of the Leominster Canal where the wharf house remains (SO668794). There is good section of the canal all the way to the Rea Aqueduct (SO651704) and there are other surviving features all the way to Leominster. The Marl Brook rises in the Stocking Pool in Mamble (SO688707) adjacent to the Mamble Colliery and it crosses part of the colliery site in a series of brick culverts. These works may have been carried out so that it could supply water to the canal.

South of Mamble Colliery, Buckets Leasow Colliery is marked by numerous shaft depressions and spoil tips either side of the road that leads to Frith Common. Further south there are more old workings in Winwrick's Wood. However this wood is dominated by the remains of twentieth century mining, mainly the efforts of the Bayton Colliery Company. By the banks of Dumbleton Brook and its tributaries are the run-in entrances of the several drift mines operated by the company. Artefacts include lengths of rail and a boiler. The tramways and roads that served these mines are still present as are a few foundations of buildings. Higher up on the bank is the site of No.3 mine and on the plateau are numerous steel tub bodies, another boiler and a compressed air receiver. Several shafts relating to Hunthouse No.8 and the Hunthouse Colliery of the Mole Brothers are still in existence; the No.12 shaft is surmounted by the original gantry and is used as an emergency water supply (SO705705). A hand windlass and sinking kibble are close by. Next to the road, at the site of Bayton No.6, the compressor house and stables have been converted to a house.

In the north of Mamble the chief features are spoil tips at Bayton No.2 (1922-1924) and Empire Colliery (1925). The unique square-section, timber-lined shaft at Bayton No.2 is now a well.

Neen Savage
At Baveney Wood there are numerous spoil tips, probably dating from the eighteenth and early nineteenth centuries. At Malpass Wood, on the west bank of Baveney Brook, are about fifty shafts, probably the site of sixteenth century ironstone workings. These are next to a large dam and it is possible that the area may once have been a bloomery, although the dam may equally be connected with the Cleobury Park blast furnace of *c.*1580, about a mile downstream the brook.

Pensax
At Penn Hall there are a number of spoil tips of *c.*1800. At Pensax Common a shaft depression (SO719694) can still be seen, and in the wood by the school there are numerous traces of old workings (SO722687). A shaft can also be found in woodland by Worles Common (SO728688). The most impressive remain is the early nineteenth-century incline leading from Pensax to Wharf Farm and the road in Stockton (SO721680).

Rock
There are still spoil tips at Old Hall, Rockmoor and Hollins. There are traces of levelled workings at Blakemoor and Gybhouse. At the Yew Tree sinking in Clows Top the manager's house and some earthworks remain. There are spoil tips at Porch Brook and at Newlands the shaft has been capped by a wind pump and is used as a water source.

Sidbury

In Hawkswood Coppice are four shafts, probably nineteenth century in date (SO705846).

Stottesdon

There are numerous old workings extending from the parish boundary with Billingsley through Chorley Covert to High Green and Harcourt. Mostly these consist of shaft depressions and spoil tips. On the Fiddle (or Ray's) brook is a bloomery (SO705832), no doubt supplied in late medieval times by nearby ironstone mines. At Harcourt there are the remains of a late eighteenth-century dam and water channel, cut to bring water to the proposed site of a hydraulic pumping engine, although the latter was never actually built (SO698829). At Harcourt there are also spoil tips and shafts of the late nineteenth-century Harcourt Colliery; the pit offices and weighbridge have been converted to a house (SO701829). In Chorley Covert a large spoil tip marks the site of Chorley drift of 1924-1929. At High Green, there are the remains of the Chorley Colliery of 1934-1939. The ruined walls of the offices and the foundations of the winding engine are obvious. Artefacts include parts of the winding wheel, boilers and the headframe, although all are now badly decayed. The northern shaft is marked by a circular depression and the site of the drift to work the top coal is an obvious hollow.

There are also a few reminders of the miners themselves in Chorley. Scott's Cottages now consist of little more than a single wall surrounded by foundations, but this was originally a pair of cottages built for workmen at the early nineteenth century mines in Billingsley (SO709836). Chorley Baptist Chapel was largely the creation of the workmen at Harcourt Colliery in 1878 (SO701833).

Elsewhere in Stottesdon, there are a few shaft depressions at Bagginswood (SO683817).

Upper Arley

On the west bank of the Severn there are spoil tips stretching southwards from Woodseaves Farm into Cherry Orchard Coppice in the Wyre Forest (SO762787). Those close to Woodseaves may be the early seventeenth century workings leased by Percival Willoughby and John Slaney from Sir Francis Lacon.

East of the Severn is Shatterford. The site of the Victorian colliery, revived in the 1930s, is still marked by spoil tips and depressions; two buildings probably date from the 1930s mine. The chief memorial to the Victorian enterprise is the Bellman's Cross Inn and the row of terraced houses facing the road, built for the workers (SO791812).

East of Brettle's Farm are two depressions in the field which mark the site of pits to work the Spirobis Limestone; the nearest thing to underground limestone working in the coalfield (SO820792). West of the farm is Arley Wood. Here there are groups of early shafts and spoil tips as well as the Arley Wood mine of the 1920s, where it is possible to make out tramways, spoil tips and the mouth of a drift. The shaft is still open.

Appendix II: List of Mines

This list contains basic details of most known collieries. However, it is not comprehensive. The post-1850 data relies heavily on the List of Mines, printed as Government Publications. These contain various errors which we have tried to eliminate, but the data should still be used with caution.

Mines, 1550-1700

Name	Lessor	Lessee	Dates	Notes
Areley Kings	Mucklows	Thomas Paramore	1622-c.1642	11 years £40 + 40tons of coal p.a.
Bayton	?	?	1609	Burial of collier
Bewdley		Ralph Clare	1624-c.1650	31 years @ 10s p.a. Ironstone
Billingsley	?	?	Medieval?	Southall Bank (SO 708840);
Chelmarsh	John Weld		1630	Trials?
	Mr Nicholas		c.1690	Burial of collier
Chetton	Thomas Hord		1594	Hollicott (SO684903)
Chorley	?	?	Medieval?	Common Heath (SO705839); Ironstone
Compton	Thomas Foley		1693	Trials
Kinlet (Earnwood)	Roland Lacon	?	1603-9?	
	Francis Lacon	?	1609-13	
		Percival Willoughby & John Slaney	1613-15	Limepit Fields (SO 750805). 9 year lease at 11d/ton the first year, then 12d/ton thereafter
	Thomas Hammond and Francis Lacon		1630	The Elves (SO735816?)
	Francis Lacon	Humphrey Wheeler	1645-c1660	
Mamble	?	?	c.1640	Westwood Farm (SO675717?)
Neen Savage	?	?	c.1600?	Malpass Wood (SO SO704775); Ironstone
Pensax	Dean & Chapter Worcester	Worcester City Corporation	1565-c.1575	
		T. Vincent	1610-?	
		Bailiff of Pensax	1641-?	12d/ton royalty
		Henry Tolley	1668-?	8d/ton royalty
Upper Arley	Francis Lacon	Percival Willoughby & John Slaney	1613-15	Bower Hill (SO758792). Terms as for Earnwood
	John Fudge		c.1608-c1628	Woodseaves? (SO760790)
	John Jennings		c.1608-c1628	Earnwood (SO755800)
	?	?	1654	Shatterford; burial of collier

Collieries 1700-1850

Location	Colliery	Lessor	Lessee	Dates
Abberley		Thomas Bury		c.1730-c1760
	Monnors			1759
	Hill Head			c.1790
	Poolhouse			1815
	Hollyacre			c.1820-1870
	Brookhouse			c.1825

Appendix II: List of Mines

Parish	Mine	Lessee	Operator	Date
	Abberley Town			c.1827
Alfrick	Upper House	John Allies	In hand	c.1755
Bagginswood	Heath Farm (SO685817)			c.1760
Bayton	Woodside (SO717743)	Blount family	Francis Bint	1761-77
	Mill	Cooke family?		c.1780
		Thomas Pearse		1829
	Almshouse Meadow			c.1830
Berrow Hill		John Allies	In hand	c.1755
Billingsley	Deserts Wood/Southall Bank (SO710840)		James Cox	c.1730-50
				c.1770
		William Pulteney	Johnson & Co.	1794-1802
			Rigby & Co	1802-5
		Lord Cleveland	Stokes & Co	1806-12
			Robert Shelton	1813-1815
	Priors Moor (SO716834)		Richard Chidley	1795-1805
Chelmarsh	Dens (SO718861)	Thomas Lewis		c.1816
Chorley	See Table			
Chetton	Eudon George			c.1765-?
	Little Scotland (SO689904)			c.1810
	Tedstill			c.1830
	Harpswood			c.1830
Cleobury	Prizeley (SO703747)			c.1830
Deuxhill	SO690875	Thomas Lewis		c.1816
Dowles	SO775764	Samuel Skey		c.1780-?
Highley	Higley Wood (SO727837)	Bernard Holland		c.1777
	New England (SO725843)			c.1785
	Rea Farm (SO747833)			c.1815
	Stanley (SO749828)	Thomas Hazelwood	John & Ben Thompson	1804-11
			William Hughes & Co	1812-24
Kingswood		Edward Cole		c.1770
Kinlet	Little Meaton (SO710787)	Thomas Purcell		c.1790
	Brook's Coppice (SO702797)	Childe family	John Fennell	1818
			Charles Holmes	1819-1821
			James Winwood	1825-1829
			Mr Freeman	1830-1831?
	Earnwood/Birch (SO737808)	Childe family	Michael Guest	1720-?
			William Lawley	c.1780-1794
			Johnson & Co.	1796-1800
Kinver	Compton (SO812841)	Mr King	Lord Stamford?	c.1830
Mamble	Southnett	Blount family		c.1720-1761
			Francis Bint	1761-1777
				1778-1925
	Newlands (SO712710)	Thomas Yates		c.1810-20
Pensax	**See table 6.1**			
Neen Savage	Baveney Wood	Mr Tolley, Benjamin Trow		c.1780-c.1850
Rock	Stildon	Richard Craddock		c.1759-c.1780
	Snead	John Craddock		c.1785
	Gybhouse			c.1825-?
	Blakemoor			c.1830
Shelsey (Great)		?		c.1742
		Stephen Wyke		c.1780
Stockton	Boughs Farm	Samuel Bray		c.1800
Trimpley	Lightmarsh (SO788769)	Samuel Haddock		c.1824
Upper Arley	Woodseaves	?		c.1750-?
	Seckley (SO772785)	Lord Valencia		c.1815
	Bromley (SO760810)			c.1830
	Pickards (SO765813)	Lord Valencia	Wagstaff family	c.1830

Collieries, 1850 to date

Format: **Name of mine**, dates worked, grid reference (if known)
Dates of individual owners (usually lessees)-
Names and dates of managers and undermanagers where recorded.
Number of men employed (underground, surface)
Average output.
Not every entry is present for all mines.

Abberley: Hollyacre/Beehive Complex c.1820-1911
i) **Hollyacre** SO747681
  c.1820-72 Norwood family
ii) **Beehive** SO745685, 746687, 750689
  1880-1908 W. Norwood.
  Undermanagers 1905 No.3 Thos Haycock, No.4 H. Bradley.
  Workforce: 1900 (17,5) 1894 (22,7) 1895 (22,5)
iii) **Beehive** (Abberley Mitre) SO748685
  1909-1911 Beehive Col. Co.
  Workforce: 1909 (6,2)

Abberley: Pool House c.1800-1894 SO730680-723687
  Lessors, Abberley Estate (c.1845-1867 Molliet Family: 1868-1894, Jones family); leased 1875 John Bailey, 1876-1881 Booth & Hardcastle, 1888-1892 James Hardcastle, 1893-1894 S. Yarnold.
  Managers 1864 Samuel Aston, 1892 Samson Yarnold.
  Workforce: 1894 (23,5)

Alveley 1935-69 SO752842
  1935-1946 Highley Mining Co., 1947-1969 NCB
  Managers 1935 H. V. Eardley, 1936-1937 C. Nicholas, 1938-1940 T.H. Stonehouse, 1941-1947 S.H. Machin, 1948-1961 R. J. Hasbury, 1961-1968 G.T. Wood, 1968-1969 E.J. Williams; Undermanagers 1937 A.E. Hemsley, 1949-1952 H. Pearce, 1953-1958 E. Morris, 1959-1961 C. Rigby, 1962-1965 G.E. Stead, 1966-1969 H. Cossey
  Workforce: 1935 (-, 9) 1937 (24,15), 1944 (619,232), 1948 (623, 191), 1950 (637, 232) 1952 (656,202) 1953 (817, 219), 1957 (892, 227), 1960 (805, 228) 1961 (730, 205), 1963 (708, 171) 1967 (543, 170), 1968 (336, 135).
  Output; 250,000 tons pa

Upper Arley: Brettles 1854-1877 SO797825
  1854-1856 Allen Wagstaff, 1856-1857 Brettles Farm Colliery Co., 1861-c.1872 Robert Jones, 1875-1877 Thomas Bertram

Upper Arley: Shatterford SO790810
  1847 Shatterford Coal & Iron Mining Company, 1848 Arley Coal, Iron Mining, Brick, Coke and Lime Company, 1850-1857 Arley Colliery Co., 1857-1861 Arley Pottery and Firebrick Company, Shatterford, 1923-1924 G. Heath, B'ham, Agent A.J. Largford, 1933-1936 Shatterford & Kidderminster Col. Co. per Straits Col. Co., Dudley. Abandoned 8/36
  Managers 1851 Henry Collinson, 1860 John Fellows, 1923 J.W. Jones, 1933-1934 H.J. Newey, 1935-1936 V. Parry
  Workforce: 1923 (2,4), 1933 sinking (9,16), 1934 (24,25), 1935 (55,20)

Arley Wood 1921-1922 SO798827
  1921 Roberts & Co., Coal Leasows, Brierley Hill. J.J. Jones manager, workforce (7,1) Closed 24 September 1921. 13 April 1922 to 17 May 1922, owner W.G. Maiden.

Areley Kings (Gladder Brook or Areley Wood) c.1850 SO793712
  Zachery Family

Bagginswood c.1860 SO682817
  Mr Robertson

Barretts Farm 1923-1926 SO730713
  1923 Old Hall Col. Co., C. Priest manager, workforce (9,2); sinking 1924, workforce (4,3), abandoned March 1925; 1926 F.J. Davies, F.E. Davies manager

Bayton: unknown 1871-1872
  James Crump

Bayton: Glebe c.1850-1874 SO692727?
  c.1850-1874 lessor Revd D. Davies; leased c.1850 Hall & Wyatt?, c.1855-c.1860 Aston & Wyatt, c.1860-1874 Thomas Wyatt & Son

Bayton: Mill c.1840-1899 SO689726
  c.1840-1899 lessor William Cook; leased 1874-1876 Broom & Hadwell, 1876-1899 William Wyatt.
  Workforce: 1894 (3,2) 1895 (3,2)

Bayton: Shakenhurst Estate
i) Worked at various sites throughout nineteenth century, lessor Wickstead family, leased 1881-1887 Jenkins Bros, 1888-1893 Tolleys & Co., 1893-1894 in hand.
ii) **Church Pits** SO691731
  W.L.Viggars. Workforce: 1894 (15,7), 1895 (10,4), 1899 (8,3)
iii) SO693735?
  1901-1903 Bayton Coal, Coke and Brick Co.
  Workforce: 1901 (4,2) 1902 (8,4)
iv) **Bayton No.1** 1904-1923 SO697734
  1904-1909 J.A. Smallshaw, Arscott Col., Shrewsbury 1910-1923 Bayton Col. Co., abandoned, October 1923
  Managers 1910-1913 F.W. Wright, 1914-1921 H. Blakemoor, 1921 A.R. Buffrey, 1922-1923 W.L. Moody; Undermanagers 1908-1909 H.S. Walshaw, 1910-1912 J.Phillips, 1913 Needham
  Workforce: 1905 (16,4) 1907 (26,5) 1913 (90,18) 1914 (91,18) 1915 (57,15), 1916 (70,18) 1922 (67,17).
  Output 17,000 tons pa.

Bayton No.2 SO690718
  1922, sinking

Bayton No.3: Hunthouse Level/Winwrick's Wood SO704699, 704701
  1924-1937 Bayton Col. Co., V. Bramall agent.
  Manager, W.L. Moody
  Workforce: 1924 (3,7), 1925 (18,12), 1926 (35,25), 1927 (35,41), 1930 (35,41), 1932 (88,49) Closed September 1937.
  Output 20,000 tons pa

Bayton No.4: Stildon Pit SO711697
  1930-1931 Bayton Col. Co.,
  Manager W.L. Moody.
  Workforce: 1930 (7,6) sinking.

Appendix II: List of Mines

Bayton No.5: New Mamble SO694714
1934-1944, Bayton Col. Co.
Managers 1934-1936 W.L. Moody, 1937-1938, A.R. Buffrey.
Workforce: 1934 (3,5) sinking, 1935 (13,11), 1936 (28,13), 1937 (81,21)
Output 15,000 tons pa

Bayton No.6 SO704700
1937-1946, Bayton Col. Co, (agents 1937-1938 V. Bramall, 1945-1948 G. Bramall). 1947-1949 Owned NCB, licensed Bayton Col Co. 1949-1950 Owned NCB. Abandoned February 1950.
Managers 1938-1948 W.L. Moody, 1949-1950 W.H. Lee.
Workforce: 1938 (3,4), 1945 (59,30), 1948 (56,25) 1949 (61,21).
Output 13,000 tons pa

Bayton No.8 Drift SO705704
1946-1950 Bayton Col. Co. & NCB, details as No.6. W.L. Moody, manager, abandoned February 1950.
Workforce: 1948 (11,4)
Output 1,500 tons pa

Bayton No.9 Drift SO7705701
1949-1950 Bayton Col. Co. & NCB, details as No.6. W.L. Moody, manager, abandoned February 1950.

Bell
1870-1872 Bell Col. Co.

Birch Hill Farm, Rock
1922-1924 J.H. Armishaw. December 1922-1924 Sinking

Billingsley 1868-1921 SO717843
1868-1875 Wm Birchley, 1876-1877 Billingsley Col. Co., 1878-1882 Severn Valley Col. Co., 1883-1910 Alfred Gibbs, 1910-1915 Billingsley Col. Co., 1916-1921 Highley Col. Co. Abandoned 31 December 1921
Managers 1879 Morgan, 1883-1894 A. Gibbs, 1895-1911 F.W. Gibbs, 1911-1915, L.E.P. Russ, 1917-1921, C.C. Nicholas; Undermanagers 1894 F.W. Gibbs, 1905-1910 G.W. Tolley, 1911-1912 S. Matthews, 1913 H. Barlow, 1914-1915 T. Halsall, 1917-1921 A. Lebeter.
Workforce: 1894 (20,4), 1895 (24,4), 1898 (25,4), 1908 (20,4), 1910 (38,280), 1911 (93,39), 1912 (74,57), 1913 (151, 87), 1915 (137,65), 1917 (117, 44), 1918 (151,42), 1919 (200,530), 1921 (219,47) Suspended September 1921
Output 40,000 tons pa

Blakemoor c.1850-1873, 1898-1899 SO725724
c.1850-1872, Lessor Davies family; leased 1859-1861 Marsh & Waterfield, 1866 Wm Dixon & Co., 1866 John Morgan. Worked 1873 William Davis. Worked 1898-1899 T.C. Dalley
Workforce: 1898 (3,2)

Buckets Leasow c.1830-1921 SO697702
c.1830-1868 in hand (Blount family), 1869-1893 Thos Aston, 1894-1921 Ed Aston Closed January 1921
Workforce: 1894 (18,8) 1895 (15,8) 1908 (12,4) 1914 (12,4) 1917 (6,3)

Chelmarsh Common
i) Assorted sites, mid-nineteenth century, worked by Winwood and Detton families, John Evans.
ii) 1881 Severn Valley Colliery Co. SO719872

Chelmarsh: Dinney Farm SO713869
Worked mid-century by Thomas Harris

Chetton: Eudon George SO693890
c.1860, worked by Blunt family

Chetton: Hollicott SO684903
1860 Samuel Walker

Chetton: Tedstill SO694880
c.1850, worked by Richard Adams/Thomas Evans
Manager James Webster

Chorley 1934-8 SO703832
1934-1936 C. & P. Blewitt, Dudley (1936 Blewitt & Sons), 1937-1938 Chorley Col. Co.
Managers 1935-1936 J.H. Humphries, 1937-1938 J.H. Newey.
Workforce: 1934 (4,4), 1935 (14,16) 1936 (45,22) 1937 (46, 18)
Output 15,000 tons pa

Chorley Drift (Woodside) 1922-1928 SO704834
1922-1924 A. Lebeter & F. Pepper, 1925-1927 Chorley Col. Co., agent F. Pepper, 1928 Chas. Home. Closed October 12 1928
Undermanagers 1923-1924 W. Turner, 1925 J. Giles, 1928 W. Turner.
Workforce: 1922 (2,2), 1923 (3,3), 1924 (8,4) 1925 (6,3) 1926 (12,2) 1928 (3,1)

Cleobury Mortimer SO758665?
1853 Henry Backhouse & Co., trial.

Compton 1859 (trial)

Eardington 1843-1860 SO713899
1843-1858 Duppa family, 1858-1860 John Hayward
Manager 1851 William Samkiss

Empire 1925 SO690718
1925 Ed. Aston

Fieldbrook 1921-1929 SO744679
i) **Nos 1, 2 and 3** 1921-1924
A.J. Jones, Abberley Estate, abandoned 13 November 1924.
Undermanager, John Whittington
Workforce: 1921 (19,14), 1922 (30,16)
ii) **No.4**, 1 January 1925-1923 May 1925
A.J. Jones, Abberley Estate
Workforce: (11,4)
iii) **Fieldbrook Slope** 1926-1 November 1926, 1927- 10 July 1928, 1929.
1926-1928 A.J. Jones, Abberley Estate; leased 1929 Hurdiss & Fletcher, Fieldbrook Col. & Brickworks
Workforce: 1927 (16,10)

Gybhouse c.1850-1894, 1922-1923 SO722728
c.1850-1872 owned W. Hanbury, c.1872-1884 worked W. Baxter, 1884-1888 W. Davies, 1889-1890 Elijah Davies, 1890-1894 F. & John Davies, 1922-1923 John Clarke. 1922 developing, 1923 suspended.

Harcourt
i) Worked at various sites in the early nineteenth century, lessor Childe family/Kinlet estate. 1856-1881 operations based at SO702828, leased to Robert Jones.
ii) SO693825 1923 Thos Halsall & Co.
Workforce (2,2)

Harpswood c.1856-1870 SO685909
1864 Edward Crump, 1864-1869 Edward Reece, 1870 in hand (John Pritchard)

Highley: Netherton SO734825?
c.1850-1855, John Davies.

Highley 1878-1969 SO747830
1878-1946 Highley Mining Co., 1947-1969 NCB. 1940-1969 worked with Alveley

157

Managers 1888 C. Lawton, 1889 W. Galley, 1890 J. Wainwright, 1891-1910. T. Bramley, 1911-1915 H.V. Eardley, 1917-1937, C.C. Nicholas, 1938-1940 T.H. Stonehouse; Undermanagers 1889 S. Wainwright, 1894-1897 A. Mosby, 1898-1910, F. Wilkes, 1911-1930, R. James, 1931 Geo Plant, 1932-1936 J.W. Thompson, 1937-1940, A.E. Hemsley.
Workforce: 1894 (137,44), 1895 (146,41), 1896 (151, 35), 1898 (204,40) 1899 (188, 40), 1900 (161,42), 1902 (200, 41), 1905 (258, 49), 1907 (277, 51), 1910 (301, 50), 1911 (340,61), 1914 (330, 61), 1915 (265, 63), 1917 (323,73), 1918 (362, 70), 1919 (378, 93), 1920 (403, 102), 1927 (404, 101) 1930 (359,127), 1932 (447, 121), 1934 (470,124), 1937, (534, 136), 1938, (562,214)
Output 150,000 tons pa

Hollins 1895-1936 SO724699
1895-1930, S. Yarnold, 1931-1936 Bayton Col. Co. Abandoned March 1936
Undermanager 1921 W.L. Moody
Workforce: 1900 (27,10), 1911 (30,13) 1914 (30,11) 1917 (30, 3), 1921 (30,14), 1927 (34,15), 1931 (37,12)
Output 10,000 tons pa

Hunthouse 1956-1972 SO704700
1956-1972 Mole Mining Co
Managers 1956-1960 W.L. Moody, 1961-1966 I. Dean-Netscher, 1967 W.L. Moody, 1968-1969 G. Hesketh. 1970-1972 J.K. Talbot
Workforce: 1957 (9,3) 1959 (33,10) 1964 (27,7) 1967 (24,7) 1970 (27,7).
Output 12,000 tons pa

Kingswood SO731773
c.1850 Mole Family, c.1860 Joseph Matthews

Kinlet (H&M) SO739819
1892-1936 Highley Col. Co.
Managers as Highley; Undermanagers 1894-1902 A. Mosby, 1904-1911 Jas. Swain, 1912-1915 Chas Davies, 1917-1936 J.E. Perry.
Workforce: 1894 (12,6) 1895 (18,21) 1896 (30,36), 1898 (122, 34), 1901 (150,39), 1904 Workforce: (240, 37), 1907 (267, 44), 1914 (262,44), 1915 (233, 32), 1917 (258, 40), 1919 (285,42), 1920 (345, 41), 1926 (282, 69), 1930 (267,72)
Output 70,000 tons pa

Mamble c.1720-1925 SO685710
To 1868 in hand (Blount family), leased 1869-1893 Thos Aston, 1894-1925 Ed Aston. Abandoned 13 December 1995.
Manager 1874 George Aston
Workforce: 1894 (9,4) 1895 (6,2), 1900(9, -), 1906 (10,4), 1920 (13,8), 1921 (18,12), 1922 (20,7)
Output 3,000 tons pa

Manor SO756710
1925-1926, A.J. Jones, Abberley Estate, agent C. Walker. Abandoned 2 October 1926
Manager 1926 A.R. Buffrey; Undermanager 1925 J. Whittington.
Workforce: 1925 (13, 6)

Neen Savage, Baveney Wood SO699790
c.1850 Owned Benjamin Trow, managed Samuel Richards

Newlands (Pensax) SO717712
1925 A.J. Jones, Abberley Estate, agent C. Walker Abandoned 31 December 1927

Manager 1926 A.R. Buffrey; Undermanager 1925 J. Whittington.
Workforce: 1925 (12, 7)

Old Hall c.1840-1900, 1928-1931 SO725721
c.1840-1875 Lessor Edward Ree, leased to Joseph Hopcutt & Co. 1856-1857. Worked 1875-1877 Joseph Ree, 1877-1881 Wm Davis, 1883-1890 Wm Bickley, 1891 Wm Bickley Jr, 1892-1893 J.R. Lindsey, 1894-1895 Lindsey & Slater, 1896 standing, 1897-1900 C. Broom, 1928 F. Mole, 1929-1931 R.G. Mole. Abandoned 21 March 1931.
Workforce: 1894 (19,4) 1895 (19,4) 1899 (2,2), 1929 (6,3), 1930 (2,1) Yard Coal worked.

Pensax Court (to 1876) SO721685, 726684, 713686, various sites on the Pensax Court Estate.
To 1862 Clutton Brock family, 1862-1876 James Higginbottom.
Managers 1851 John Craddock, 1872 Emmanuel Millichip
Output 3,000 tons pa

Pensax Common SO690720
1895 Charles Potter

Pensax: Penn Hall SO714690
c.1840-1855 William Barnbrook, 1877-1881 Lessor John Knott, leased to Lewis Bros

Porchbrook Drift (Abberley) SO726707
1926-1927 A.J. Jones, Abberley Estate, Abandoned 30 September 1927
Manager 1926-1927 A.R. Buffrey.
Workforce: 1926-1927 (30,8)

Rock 1907-1909
Alfred Sidney. No coal worked.

Rockmoor (H&M) SO727714
Lessor Fred Rogers; 1876-1881 in hand, 1890 Thomas Byng, 1891 George Mole, 1892 Barlow & Powitt, 1892-1894 J. & E. Whitehouse, 1894-1896 Rockmoor Coal & Coke Co., 1896-1898 T.C. Dalley (1897-1898, H. Johnson, agent)
Manager 1895 J. Whitehouse.
Workforce: 1894 (34,23) 1895 (53,16), 1896 (29,6)

Snead
February 1906 A.J. Davies
Workforce: February 1906 (4,2)

Tasley SO699942
1872-1875 T. Cartwright. 1888 standing.

Upper Snead SO732698
1910 January-September Beehive Col. Co. No coal extracted.

Winwoods SO734775
December 1922-May 1923, 1926-1927 Edwin Tolley. Abandoned 27 May 1927
Manager 1926 W. Turner, 1927 Edwin Tolley
Workforce: 1926 (3,2)

Yew Tree SO718719
1898-1899 T.C. Dalley, sinking
Workforce: 1898 (5,5)

Constructed from List of Coal Mines, (using data from returns for 1854-1881, 1888-1915, 1917-1938, 1945, 1948, 1950) supplemented with other records where available. Owners noted from 1856, men from 1894.

Index

Numbers in **bold** include illustrations.

Abberley 13, 17, 18, 23, 115-119, 136, 150, 154, 156

Accidents 36, 40-3, 59, 61-2, 65, 75, 83, 93, 99, 104, 111, 117-8, 120-2, 128

Aerial ropeways **92-4**, **106-7**, 128-**30**, 131

Alveley **6**, 11,16, **27-31**, 33, 35, 43, **45-6**, 56, 99-110, 140, 143-4, 150, 156

Areley Kings 18, 23, 70, 150, 154, 156

Arley (Upper) 18, 27, 36, 40, 62, 65, 66, 68, 69, 153, 155, 156

Aston family (Mamble) 39, **126**-8, 134, 136, 156-8

Bagginswood (Stottesdon) 75, 153, 155, 156

Barretts Farm Colliery (Rock) 122, 156

Bayton **11**,13, 24-**5**, 27, 29, 45, 52-**6**, 58, 118, 122, 127-34, 143, 150, 154-7

Baxter, William 121

Belgian miners 94-5

Bertram, Thomas 69

Bewdley 13, 40, 70, 80, 91, 115, **137**, 154

Bickley, William 121

Billingsley 16-20, 22-3, **25**, **29**, 33, 35, 37, 39, 49, 54, 55, 61, 66, 71-2, 74-5, 77-**85**, 90-6, 121, 144, 150-1, 154-6

Birch Farm 13, 15, 66, 78, 151, 155

Birchley family (Billingsley) 82, 156

Blakemoor 40, 120, 122, 155-6

Blewitt family 75-**6**, 157

Blount family (Mamble) 19, 24, 27, 73-4, 125-8, 131, 155

Bramall family (Bayton) 128, 131, 139-40

Bray family (Pensax) 111-3, 155

Bridgnorth 13, 17, 20, 43, 66, 84, 87, 107, 110

Brickworks 20, 59-62, 67-8, 70, 92-3, 117, 119-122

Brock Hall coal 13, 15, 18, 123,

Brooch coal 16, 75, 89, 104, 107

Broom family (Bayton) 121, 127-8

Browning family (Pensax) 112-4

Buckets Leasow Colliery (Mamble) 31-**2**, 125-7, 157

Byng, Thomas 121

Caffin & Co. 92-3

Chelmarsh 6, 13, 19, 18, 40, 43, 59, 61, 151 154-5

Chetton 17, 50, 59-60, 151, 154-5

Childe family () 66, 74, 78, 80-1, 87, 90, 123, 155 Kinlet

Chorley 2, 17-8, 27, 69, 71-2, 75-**6**, 153-5, 157

Clee Hills (including Charlecotte) 19, 39, 44, 69, 71, 77, 84

Cleobury Mortimer 4, 8, 55, 63, 71, 128, 155, 157

Clutton (Brock) family (Pensax) 19, 20, 111-5, 158

Coal cutters 29-**30**, 90, 96-9, 108, 140

Collinson, Henry 50, 68, 156

Compressed air 29-**30**, 69, **76**, 128, 131, 136, 138, 140, **142**

Compton 20, 67, 152, 154-5, 157

Cook family (Bayton) 127, 156

Cooke, Robert 112-3

Cox, James 71, 73, 77

Craddock family (Pensax) 39, 73-4, 112-3, 155, 158

Crump, Edward 59

Crump family (Chorley) 71-4

Dalley, Thomas 122, 157-8

Davies, Rev David 127

Davies family (Blakemore) 120

Davis, William 120-1

Dimbleby, Samuel 83-4

Deuxhill 13, 59, 60, 155

Dowles and Far Forest 16, 70, 123, 155

Duppa family (Eardington) 60-1, 157

Eardington Colliery 60-1, 85, 151, 157

Eardley, Harry 99

East Shropshire Coalfield 18-9, 39, 49, 54-5, 61, 65-6, 71-3, 80, 110

Electricity 29-31, 33, 45, 58, 69, 90, 92, 96-100, 104, **109**, 123, 139-41

Empire Colliery 134-**5**, 157

Eudon George 60, 151, 155, 157

Evans family (Highley) **11**, **38**

Fellows, John 68-9, 156

Fieldbrook Colliery (Abberley) 119, 150, 157

First aid teams 40, **41-2**, **94**

Findlay John 53-4

Gasification at Rock 123-**4**

Gibbs family (Billingsley) **29**, 84-**5**, 93, 156

Gybhouse Colliery (Rock) 43, 121-2, 155, 157

Hanbury, William 121

Hann, Edmund 90

Harcourt 21, 71 73-5, 85, 153, 157

Hard Mine Coal 13, 15, 16, 117, 119, 131, 138-9, 144

Hardcastle, James (Abberley) 118, 156

Harpswood 59-60, 155, 157

Hasbury, Ray 104, 143

Hazeldine, William 80-1

Highley (village and mines) 6, 22-4, **26**-7, 31, 33, 36-7, **39**-40, **43**, 45-7, 50, 51, 52, 53, 54, 55, 56, 58, 75-**6**, 78-80, 85-7, 90, 92-101, 104, 128, 143, 151, 155, 157-8

Higginbottom, James 115, 123, 158

Hollicott 17, 59, 60, 154, 157

Hollins Colliery (Pensax) **52**, 118, 135-6, 158

Hopcutt, Joseph (Rock) 120, 158

Hord, Thomas (Bridgnorth) 17, 154

Horses 28-**9**, 31, 44, 47, 81, 104

Hunthouse Colliery (Bayton No 6) 136-40, 157-8

Hunthouse Colliery (Mole Mining Co.) 28, 33, 124, 140-**2**, 158

Hughes, William (Stanley) 62-4, 155

Ironworks 17-9, 62, 65, 71, 77, 80-2, 114-5

Johnson, George (Newcastle) 72-4, 77-80, 155

Johnson, Henry (mining engineer) 84, 122

Jones, Daniel 16, 60

Jones family (Abberley) 118-9, 156-8

Jones, Robert 69, 74-5

Kingswood 67, 155, 158

Kinlet 16-8, **23**-4, 27-8, **32**, **35**, **48**, 55, 65, 66, 67, 75, 87-90, **96**-9, 101, 112, 123, **144**-5, 151-5, 158

Kinver 16, 28, 152, 154-5

Lacon family (Kinlet) 65, 66, 154

Lebeter, Arthur (Billingsley) 75, 157

Leominster Canal 19, 112, 114, 123, 125

Limeworks 16-7, 62, 67-8, 115, 117

MacNab, Henry Gray 49-50, 77, 79-80, 155

Main Sulphur Coal 13, 15, 16, 20, 62, 122, 131, 138-9, 144

Mamble 18-9, 31, 33, 52, 54, 125-7, 131, 134, 136, 152, 154-5, 158

Manor Colliery (Rock) 119, 158

Mellor, William 82-4

Mole family (Clows Top) 121-2, 134-5, 140-2, 158

Murchison, Sir Roderick 16, 21

National Coal Board 27, 104-10, 124, 140, 142

Neen Savage (Baveney and Malpass Woods) 17, 50, 71, 75, 152, 154-5

Newcastle on Tyne 10, 62, 77

New Mamble Colliery **30**, 136-9, 158

Newlands Colliery (Mamble) 119, 125, 158

Norwood family 115-117, 155-7

Old Hall Colliery (Rock) 50, 120-2, 155, 158

Old Hall Bats 13, 15, 119, 135, 144

Paramore, Thomas 70

Pearson, E.J. & J. Ltd 135

Pelley, Commander Richard 68

Pensax 17, 18, 19, 20, 23, 33, 40, 43, 46, 52, 54, 111-5, 152, 154-5, 158

Porchbrook Colliery (Abberley) 119, 158

Poyner family (Highley) **44**, **48**

Pritchard, John 59-60

Pulteney, William (MP) 77-8, 81, 155

Quarries 62, 80, 93

Railways and tramways 10, 19-20, 23, **31**, 61-2, 65-6, 74, 78-80, 82, 84, **87**, **89**-93, 100-**2**, 104, 115, 121-2, 125, 128, **130**, 133

Ree family (Rock) 50, 120, 158

Reece, Edward 59

Rigby, Thomas 81

Rock 24, 119, 122, 152, 155, 158

Rockmoor 119, 121-**4**, 158

Rogers, Frederick 121

Severn, River 13, 18-20, 62-4, 77-80

Shakenhurst Colliery (Bayton), 127-8, 134-5, 156

Shatterford 16, 21, 27, 29, 50, 67-**70**, 74, 153-4, 156

Shaw, Sir Joseph 90

Shrewsbury Coalfield 111, 128

Sidbury 72, 153

Slaney, John 65-6, 154

Salter, Alexander 120-1

Smallshaw, James 128, 156

Snead (Rock) 119, 122, 128, 158

South Staffordshire Coalfield 19-21, 39, 50, 53, 56, 64, 68-9, 80-1, 104, 108, 110, 122-3, 135, 140

Stanley Colliery (Highley) 20-1, 33, 49, 62-4, 155

Steam engines **2**, **32**-3, 59-60, 64, 75, 81-2, **91**, **97**-**8**, 112, 115-8, 120-1, 127, **132**-**3**, 136, 139

Stildon (Pensax) 112, 119, 135-6, 155, 158

Stokes, George 80-1, 155

Stonehouse family (Highley) 28, **41**, 45, **144**, 157

Stottesdon 153

Stourport 62, 102, 107

Tasley 158

Taylor, George 84

Taylor, Samuel 82-3

Tedstill 60, 157-8

Telford, Thomas 20, 77, 80

Thompson, John and Benjamin (engineers) 19, 20, 62, 155

Thompson, John (solicitor), 82-4

Tolley family **85**, 111, 156-7

Trade tokens 63

Trevithick, Richard 82

Unions 50-**8**, 94, 140

Ventillation 75, **88**, **93**, **95**, 99, 104, 141

Viggars family (North Staffs) 85, 128, 156

Wagstaff family (Arley) 67, 69, 155

Ward family (Alveley Colliery) **37**

Water power and drainage 33, 64, 67, 70, 72-5, 77, 81-2, 86, 115, 121, 125, 131, **135**-6, 140, 142

Weld, John (Willey) 61, 155

Weston, John 71

Westwood family (Alveley Colliery) **38**

Whitehouse, J. & E. (Coseley) 121

Wiggan, Thomas 69

Willoughby, Sir Percival 65-6, 154

Winwood family 39, 50, 155, 157

Winwoods Colliery (Kinlet) 67, 151, 155, 158

Winwrick's Wood Colliery (Bayton No 3) 27, **34**, 131-**4**, 136-9, 157

Worcester 17, 62-4, 87, 111

Wright, F.W. 128, 156, 158

Wyatt family (Bayton) 127-8, 156

Yarnold, Samson (Pensax) 46, 50, **52**, 118, 135, 156, 158

Yew Tree Colliery (Clows Top) 122, 158